Money,
Power,
Respect

What Brothers Think,
What Sistahs Know

Also by Denene Millner and Nick Chiles

The Sistahs' Rules
By Denene Millner

What Brothers Think, What Sistahs Know
By Denene Millner and Nick Chiles

What Brothers Think, What Sistahs Know About Sex
By Denene Millner and Nick Chiles

Money, Power, Respect

What Brothers Think, What Sistahs Know

Denene Millner and Nick Chiles

William Morrow

An Imprint of HarperCollins*Publishers*

HarperCollins books may be purchased for educational, business, or sales promotional use. For information please write: Special Markets Department, HarperCollins Publishers Inc., 10 East 53rd Street, New York, NY 10022.

FIRST EDITION

Designed by Michael Mendelsohn
ISBN 0-688-17886-3

**To our parents,
our muse**

Contents

Acknowledgments ix

Introduction xi

Part I Money

1 Can He Deal When She Makes More? 3

2 One Saves, the Other Spends:
Can This Household Ever Have Peace? 14

3 Keeping Money Secrets 24

4 Food, Fun, and Incidentals: Does He Always
Have to Pay? 37

5 Help Wanted: What Happens When He's Out of Work? 48

6 Pre-Nups 63

Part II Power

7 Does Money Equal Power? 77

8 Chores and Child-Rearing: Can They Ever Be
Equally Divided? 89

9 In Corporate America: Does It Matter Who's on Top? 106

10 Work Time vs. Face Time: Which Is More Important? 119

Contents

11 Whose Word Wins—Your Spouse's or Your Family's?   132

12 Ending It: Does It Matter Who Initiates the Breakup?   143

Part IIII   Respect

13 Hello?: Why Isn't He Listening to Me?   157

14 Whose Career Is More Important?   167

15 Infidelity: Should I Tell My Spouse?   180

16 Arguing: Does Someone Always Have to Win?   191

17 Dirty Laundry: How Much Do We Air to Friends
    and Family?   201

18 Who You Calling a Bitch?: Does It Matter
    How We Talk to Each Other?   213

Acknowledgments

We have many partners in these bookwriting endeavors who make the whole process silky smooth and sometimes even a lot of fun. Of course, we must begin with our families—our parents, siblings, and close friends. We can't tell you enough how much we love you.

In the final analysis, it is for our children, Mazi and Mari, that we do what we do. If we can make a difference and cause them to have a moment's less pain, then it will have been profoundly worthwhile.

Our wonderful and gracious editor, Kelli Martin, rode in like a one-woman cavalry just in the nick of time to save us from despair. We think our agent, Victoria Sanders, must have been sent to us by angels; on second thought, perhaps she's a member of the angel guild herself. We offer a hearty thanks to Eileen Cope for all her work on our behalf.

Introduction

Want to clear out a room in a hurry? Ask a few married couples if they keep money secrets from each other, or if the husband contributes enough to household chores, or whether the husband's or the wife's career is deemed more important in the relationship. These are the sticky questions that go unanswered in relationships, the ground zero issues that couples evade like skilled boxers—feinting, bobbing, and weaving to stay out of the line of fire. But even if we think we're successfully avoiding them, they never really go away. Issues of money, power, and respect simmer at the core of every relationship, influencing the way we respond to every crisis, manipulating the behaviors we exhibit each moment of our lives together. But instead of addressing them, facing them head-on, we let our assumptions rule the day. Rather than asking questions, we allow the anger and the frustration to build—sometimes without even realizing where the anger and frustration are coming from.

Perhaps the reason we seek to avoid talking about money, power, and respect is because we know how crucial these issues are to our relationship's survival. Evasion is always a whole lot easier than confrontation. But who ever said relationships were supposed to be easy?

During the course of writing this book, we made a discovery: The more you talk about this stuff, the easier it becomes to talk about it. A few times we even had fun. Imagine that, having fun arguing about whether the road is harder for black men or black women in corporate America, and why women always assume their spouses will pay for the food, fun, and incidentals when we're out together.

Of course, the flip side of our discovery is that the more you avoid talking about money, power, and respect, the harder it becomes, the more distress it causes, the more bitter are the disputes. If the husband has always assumed his career had top priority in the household, he might get a painful jolt when his wife comes home and announces that they must move to a new state because she just got a promotion. If the wife always figured that the husband would want her to confess every little flirtatious indiscretion with a member of the opposite sex—because she'd want him to confess the same—she might be shocked at his reaction when she tearfully reveals to him that she kissed a co-worker.

Money is the ebola virus of relationships—with frightening speed, it can push a solid, healthy relationship to its deathbed, blood flowing from every orifice as the internal organs and major systems turn to mush. And like ebola, money woes slice through communities and leave a path of pain and devastation in their wake—along with long lines at the divorce court. If there's one thing we would love for couples to get out of this book, it's a greater willingness to talk about money, to dig into each partner's money fears and money expectations until the dread starts to melt away. That's the only way to tame the virus.

When we talk to audiences, power issues always seem to lead to hostile debate. Some brotherman will stand up and proclaim that "the problem with black women is y'all refuse to acknowledge that the man is supposed to have the power in the relationship." Then the brother will sit down with a satisfied smile—and all hell will break loose. It will take minutes to restore order as the curse words start to recede and the fingers are pried away from the brother's throat. His voice hoarse, his pulse weak, the brother will say, "See, that's what I'm talking about." We don't pretend that black men and black women will agree on questions of power, but we believe this is a conversation that we need to have if we're going to get at the roots of the hostility that brothers and sistahs carry around. What determines who will have more power in the relationship—is it the person who makes more money, or is it always the man? Does it even matter?

This leads us to the question of respect. Though the other issues may be more controversial and explosive, this one is clearly the most important. Respect must be the foundation upon which any solid relationship is built—whether between a man and a woman, or employer and employee, or parent and child. In the African-American community, if you watch music videos and daytime talk shows and listen to music lyrics, you'll quickly discover that respect between men and women is in drastically short supply right now. Some might conclude it's nonexistent. We can screw each other, ogle each other, fight with each other, curse at each other, but the last thing we seem to do is respect each other. Psychologists might say we first need to respect ourselves before we can earn respect from anyone else, but that response is too easy, too pat. It's right up there with "you have to love yourself before anyone else will love you"—and we know that's not necessarily true. No, there is something deeper going on in this raging war between the sexes in our community—a lack of understanding, a lack of communication, a lack of empathy. The result is a lack of respect. Maybe if we start talking about it, we can lower the hostility and spread some love. Long before Lil' Kim and The Lox told us in a rap song that money, power, and respect were what we needed in life, Aretha Franklin spelled it out for us. R-E-S-P-E-C-T.

Part I

Money

1

Can He Deal
When She Makes More?

From a Sistah

I'm just confused.

Because the gold digger is supposed to be the sistah that doesn't have jack bone and looks to the man to give her the ring, the house, the car, the credit cards, the furs, the clothes, the trips—the everything. She, rightfully, is avoided like the plague by the brothers.

Y'all know what I'm talking about; guys can spot her quicker than an NBA player can an unbeweavable, bought-it-at-Mandee hootchie/groupie standing outside the hotel talking 'bout how she just happened to be there on business and "Whaddaya know? I ran into my favorite baller!"

He can't stand the gold digger. Wants to get as far away from her as humanly possible. Will run from her like a black girl in a scary horror flick. Won't stick around to see the gruesome details—or become one. Will simply break out at the first sight of blood.

And who can blame him? I mean, we got-it-goin'-on sistahs want to beat her ass down, too, because she's giving a really bad image to us new millennium women—the ones who know that in the Y2K1 you have to bait your own line, catch your own damn fish, and cook that bad boy, too. Shoot, can't always depend on some man to feed you, because there might come a day when you're going to be really hungry, and boyfriend's little worm just won't snag a thing but some stinky, old (inedible) rubber boots. Not to mention that the first time he even remotely thinks we're depending on him for those material things, he's going to label us gold diggers—which we know we're not.

So we toil and slave and pray and slave some more, trying our best to get the house, the car, the credit cards, the furs, the clothes, the trips—the everything—for ourselves. The only thing we really look for from you all is the ring, and in return, we offer you the promise that though we will not depend on you for the finer things, we will appreciate the fact that you can provide them.

This, we figure, should make the gold digger–hating brothers happy. Really happy. Because you all have the best of both worlds; a woman who is not only capable of making her own money, but isn't jocking you for yours. You don't have to worry about spending all your little money on our playthings; we'll get those for ourselves. And we'll make sure that there's plenty left over so that you can relax a bit, too—so you won't have to worry about scrimping and scratching and killing yourselves to keep us living in the style to which we're accustomed. We can do all that scratching together.

Alas, you all are not happy with that kind of sistah. At least you don't appear to be. You avoid her much like you do the gold digger, except the sistah with money in her pocket just doesn't get why. She is shunned, spat on, dragged through the dirt in the brothers' court of law. In his eyes, she has a big mouth. She is emasculating. She is unfeminine. She is a bra-burning feminist. She has a big mouth. She is a bitch.

Or at least that's the way you all treat her.

Just because she has the nerve to make a good living.

This, of course, is especially disappointing to the sistah who studied, worked hard, climbed the corporate ladder, then looked around and realized there weren't that many brothers up there with her at the top. After years of trying really hard to find a man who could bring an equal amount—or perhaps more—to the table, she revises her standards on her "My Man Must Have" list, scratching off the "must have money" requirement. We start re-thinking what it is we want in a man, and finally decide that it's okay if he's a blue-collar brother netting half what we're bringing home. We decide it's okay if he's only read about the places we've been to. Shoot, at some point, some of us sistahs get so desperate for companionship that we are willing to overlook the fact that brotherman can't even read.

And then we get into a relationship with a blue-collar/ain't-been-nowhere/barely-cleared-his-GED-requirements brother, and he decides he's going to break out because he can't stand that she makes more money than him.

Huh? What the hell is that?

Why do men get all worked up when a woman makes more than them?

From a Brother

Boy, you ladies sure like to talk about this one, don't you? It seems that women who don't have a man or any prospects need to find some explanation for it, and this is usually the one that gets trotted out, a handy-dandy all-inclusive rationale for female loneliness. If

*you are spending time with a lot of brothers who flee when they dis-
cover you make more money, you are simply picking the wrong men.
These are troubled brothers just looking for an excuse to get out of
the relationship. The rest of us, the stable, confident brothers, we
stick around.*

What it all comes down to is confidence. That word shouldn't
be confused with *ego*. *Confidence* means that we are certain of our
abilities, our worth, our accomplishments, our attractiveness, even
if we aren't the highest-earning brother on the block. It means that
we don't glean our sense of self merely from the size of our bank
account. This is an important attribute for brothers to have in this
land of unequal opportunity because we do have much difficulty
being placed in the positions where we can bring home long, wide,
and thick cash. It's kind of like the discovery social psychologists
made that black girls in the United States have a much better self-
image than white girls because they instinctively realize the folly
of using the beauty standards of white society to form their own
sense of self. Similarly, black men know that they have to look beyond their wallets to form their self-image. Sometimes the places
we look aren't as helpful to our long-term interests—basketball-
playing abilities, street toughness, musical talent—but they do give
us a sense of self that is completely divorced from our position in
the marketplace.

The ego is tapped when we are comparing ourselves to others,
figuring out where we stand. Brothers without a lot of confidence,
without an internal strength that doesn't wither depending on
which way the winds blow, will have their egos crushed by a successful, striving sistah who appears to be on top of the world. They
will constantly feel an incessant need to compare themselves to
her, to see how they measure up. And of course they will forever

come up far short. Like Muggsy Bogues trying to wear Shaq's pants, it will be obvious to anyone who looks that the brother is out of his league. This is when the Ax Men spring into action. They get to chopping to cut that woman down to their size, to bring her down a few notches so that they won't feel so inferior. Criticize her, insult her, berate her, maybe even hit her. All to protect their fragile little egos. You can't help but be saddened by the sight of it, and you do see it all the time.

A confident brother can be a garbageman, a custodian, an air-conditioning repairman. It really doesn't matter. He doesn't define himself by his paycheck. He doesn't need letters at the end of his name to know that he's an intelligent, interesting, witty, and attractive man. His mother raised him to be warm, sensitive, and self-sufficient. To not be afraid of women. If his father was around, he showed him how to treat women with respect and adoration. To not feel the constant need to compare yourself to your woman to gauge your accomplishments. To be a real man.

We real men are out here, watching the women with the Ax Men and shaking our heads. We may not be the most abundant creatures on the planet, but you can find us if you keep looking. Check out that friendly looking brother over there in the corner, the one who isn't wearing the flashiest suit in the room, the one who doesn't need to dominate every conversation. He's having a good time in his quiet, unassuming way; he knows that he belongs at the party and doesn't have to prove it to everyone within earshot. He wants to talk to people truly to learn more about them, not to tell them how much he has or to find out if they have more. A lot of women will overlook that brother and gravitate toward the louder brother with the nicer suit, not realizing that the nicer suit is all about the show, the put-on as self-promotion. If he needs to advertise his worthiness, that should be a loud, shrill warning bell to every woman in the room. Nice suit is the dangerous brother. He's the potential Ax Man. Keep walking, over to the corner.

Once you get into a relationship with the confident brother, it's necessary to accept him for what he is. That means you can't start hoping he transforms himself into Earl Graves.

Deep down, though, don't women think a man is somewhat lame if his woman makes more than he does?

From a Sistah

Sure, some do. Guaranteed, though, these women wouldn't give you the time of day in the first place, so you don't have to worry about what they're thinking, anyway. You can rest assured that the sistah who disregards your paycheck has long ago reconciled in her mind that she's not bothered by it, and has recognized that there are so many more reasons to be with a man than to live without him over something stupid like his making less money than her.

Let's be for real: Society—not just women—cocks a critical eye on the brother who dares to date or marry a woman who clocks more dollars than he. In fact, I've heard more men criticize such unions than I ever have women. Admit it: How many times have you heard guys poke fun at Stedman for hanging in there with Oprah? Or question just what it is that Rohan Marley does for a living while his wife, soulster Lauryn Hill, rakes in all that dough from her Grammy award–winning works? Or assume that Susan Taylor's husband is pimping his wife's fame to further his own writing aspirations? Or made fun of Iyanla Vanzant's husband for getting in on the motivational speaking and writing craze after having seen what it did for his wife's career?

We women don't tend to pay it too much mind. Shoot, we don't really care that Stedman makes hundreds of thousands and his honey makes hundreds of millions; we just want to be the first to know when he slips a ring on her finger and says the two magic words, "I do." We don't question what Rohan is doing for a living; we beam when, at the awards ceremonies, the camera cuts to him and he smiles after his honey picks up another statue and thanks her man for being a wonderful companion and daddy. Same thing for Susan, particularly when she takes the dais and says that she is at peace and in love with her husband—just the way a happy couple should be.

I'm sure this issue is not easy for any of these couples to deal with. Their names are constantly in the newspapers and on the radio and on the television and on people's lips. And everyone feels like they have the right to comment on their affairs—whether it be their love affairs or their business affairs—making it extremely difficult, I'd surmise, for them to settle down for the night and enjoy each other's company without first having to excise all the negativity spewed against their partners during the course of a day.

Nick and I even went through this when *The Sistahs' Rules* first hit the bookshelves. While I was going on national television shows and traveling across the country promoting my book on radio and in newspapers, all his boys were ribbing him, calling him "Stedman" and "Mr. Millner." It was always, like, the first thing out of their mouths when they saw the two of us together, much to Nick's chagrin. He didn't like it. At all. To this day, when we go to a hotel, boyfriend will flip if we're registered under my name and the concierge deigns to call him "Mr. Millner" instead of "Mr. Chiles."

None of my girlfriends did this to him. None of them remotely wondered whether I would leave my man now that I had a coupla extra dollars and a book in the store. To them, my fortune was the Chiles family's fortune—nothing more, nothing less. It didn't make Nick any less of a man; in fact, it made him more the man because his wife was blowing him up all throughout her book.

This is the way, I think, a lot of sistahs look at it. They understand that a woman who dates or marries a man who makes less money than she has moved way past what's in his wallet, and has trained her radar on the kind of person he is. So what if he drives a truck. He brings that money right on home, helps with the bills, treats her right, is a good daddy to her children, is a moral, righteous individual, is capable of holding stimulating conversation, knows how to please her in every possible way—all the things she's ever looked for in a mate. His money—or the lack thereof—isn't going to be the deciding factor as to whether she's going to go for it or not. Certainly, it may be one of the factors, but it won't be a deal-breaker if she's got her head on straight.

I think the thing that makes unions like this lame is when the man's insecurities get in the way. His ego, which has for so long depended upon the notion that he has to have a better job than his woman, make more money than his woman, have a higher position of authority than his woman—be an all-around more valued worker than his woman—will force him out of the relationship. He's the one who just can't take it, and ultimately, he is the one who will decide that it's just not going to work out. But it will always be her fault—never his. She will be the self-serving, money-hungry, wanna-be-the-man chick he will loudly proclaim to his boys he just couldn't get with. "She's just high maintenance," he'll say. "I do enough maintenance at work—ain't trying to come home and buff, too."

This, of course, is completely unfair to her, because all she wanted to do was live the good life: have a good career and a good man. And, as usual, he won't let it happen.

Perhaps it's not like this for every man, but if I've seen it happen once, I've seen it a thousand times. Answer me this:

Would she have to give up her good job and high salary to keep you, or is there a way for you to get over it?

From a Brother

If you are even considering leaving a good job and high salary to keep a man, you need to beat yourself hard about the face and head a few times. You don't need a different, lesser job—what you need is a new man.

Now I know there are many sistahs walking around out there telling everybody that black men just can't handle a sistah's success. But the brothers who are guilty of that kind of weakness certainly don't need their pathetic lameness affirmed and justified by a woman deciding to take an inferior job on their behalf. That's so despicable it makes my blood boil just thinking about it. We all need to rise above that kind of petty smallness. Under no circumstances is that a move that will gain you anything but heartache, anger, and a lot of overdue credit card bills.

Relationships are supposed to be affirming, liberating. They are supposed to help us reach for the best part of us, to help each of us become the embodiment of everything God wanted us to be. The man you described as attacking his woman if she makes more and is more accomplished is obviously a brother with a serious cardboard ego—it's all a front, erected from the thin, flimsy stuff of shoe boxes and milk cartons. Even the slightest bit of pressure will lead to collapse, and any woman nearby will be in danger of getting smashed.

When things got unbearable for me at the last newspaper where I worked, it was my wife who suggested that I walk away from the newspaper business and write books full-time. It was a show of faith on her part that didn't come without a bit of soul-searching on the part of both of us as to whether we were financially and mentally ready to be that self-sufficient. But the beauty of it was that she understood the anguish the job was causing me, she knew what would make me happy, and she nudged me in that direction knowing that it had the potential to make our financial straits a bit tighter. It was a partner-affirming decision and I will always treasure her for having the strength to make it—a strength I know every woman out there doesn't possess. The decision is paying off for her and me as it continues to lead to more wonderful moments in our writing careers. I tell myself over and over that I should never take this woman for granted.

That's what partners are supposed to do for each other when it comes to careers. We're supposed to nudge each other—or kick each other in the behind—to make the moves that will lead to even greater success and self-fulfillment. We're not supposed to force our women to do things that will make us feel better about ourselves or make us look better by comparison.

Admittedly, there are brothers out there who need to gaze into a mirror and make sure they are providing their partners with this kind of affirming and self-sacrificing support. It's tempting to get into this game of blaming someone else for our failures or shortcomings. Sometimes African Americans become a little too practiced at this art. But when we are sitting down across the table from the woman we love, we must be able to look her in the eye and tell her we have done everything we could to help her succeed at home and in the workplace. And she should be able to say the same thing to us. If she happens to be bringing home more cheese, why does it have to be a statement about the male? Maybe a better way to consider the situation would be to believe her success is instead a reward for the talent and ambition of the female.

Of course, there's one thing in this scenario that I've accepted on faith: that the woman hasn't been torturing the brother with her superior career accomplishments. By this I mean holding it over his head like a guillotine poised to zoom downward every time he gets out of line. The brother in that relationship would have no choice but to grow resentful of his woman's success, because she's practically begging him to do so. What qualifies as torture? Lots of speeches like the following: "Why don't you just go in to your boss and demand that he put you on that special project? No way I would accept anything less at my job. When they wouldn't give me the promotion I wanted, I demanded it. Now look how far I've gone."

If this sounds like you, then you probably need to find another method of motivating your man, 'cause it's only a matter of time before he rears up and tells you where to stick that wonderful job of yours.

One Saves, the Other Spends: Can This Household Ever Have Peace?

From a Sistah

S hoes. And baby clothes. And cooking and entertainment utensils.

They are my vices.

I could have just enough money in my account to pay my bills, and a little extra for savings, and savings will inevitably get kicked to the curb when I stroll up into Saks and see those bad pink Donna Karan mules, the ones with the really cute, petite bow across the arch and the funky, pointed heel. Or when I go to the third floor in Bloomingdale's and see all those pretty Little Me dresses and the OshKosh B'Gosh jackets and Donna Karan suits in stunning grays and maroons and pea greens—my daughter Mari's colors. Or when I pass by the window of any kitchen appliance store on earth, and see all the beautiful serving platters and big, sunken pots and cooking gadgets. I get to thinking about the kind of dinner party I could throw, having cooked all my food in that new saucepan, and served it in my new mules with Miss Mari on my hip in her new little outfit.

Oh, I'm much better than I used to be; at least I'm paying my bills. When I was in college and shortly thereafter, I would go without eating, much less paying bills, to buy clothes and kitchen stuff—which is why my credit was jacked up for so long. But dammit, I looked good and so did my food.

Mommy's probably going to kick my booty for writing this, but I think I took after her in the spending department. For as long as I can remember being able to remember, my mom has never let her finances get in the way of her having nice things. I can recall having a really nice relationship with Mr. UPS man, who would find his way to my parents' house at least once every other day, bearing brown bundles full of pantsuits and beautiful dresses and cozy winter coats. My mom would come home from work and rip the boxes open, put on her new outfits, and twirl around in front of her mirror. Simply beautiful. She was happy like a kid under the Christmas tree—except her fa la la la las were coming year 'round.

I also remember my father being pretty perturbed by the fact that while my mom struggled to pay all those credit card bills run up by her catalogue fetish, he was paying the water, heat, and electric bills, the car notes, the insurance, the mortgages, and every other living expense the two of them had, plus his little credit card bills and other incidentals. He was the money worrywart—the one who, if he had two pennies left over, would put both of them in the savings account "for that rainy day." This was his credo; one never knew what tomorrow was going to bring, so you better put your money away in case some stuff breaks out.

My mom's motto?

Ya can't take it with you.

I'd like to think that today, I'm a pleasant mixture of the two of them. I'm free-spending like my mom—will not deny myself or my daughter the finer things in life just because the bank account is a little low. But I'm also anal like my dad—will get really uneasy if the bank account is low, and will do what it takes to get it back to a stable level, so that I don't get caught with my pants down in case of an emergency.

Still, I'm sure that when Nick sees the American Express bill, he's not all that happy about the way-too-many charges at Baby Gap and Crate & Barrel.

I get the feeling that he's not the only brother who feels this way, and I'm not the only sistah who spends this way.

We agree that if there is a genuine need for us to save some money for that inevitable rainy day, we certainly won't mind stashing a little cash for the occassion. Still, I have to agree with my mom on one key issue: Ya can't take it with you. We sistahs like to enjoy ourselves, look good, step lively. We want the same for our kids. The bills will get paid—eventually.

Somehow, though, you all don't seem to think we're capable of such ventures. So I ask you this:

Why do you all get so worked up when we use money for what it was meant for—spending?

From a Brother

As you described, so much of our views on spending and household finances comes from our parents and the way we were raised that it almost seems as if we have no control over them. That's admittedly a scary notion, but one that we should keep in mind the next time we feel like we want to body slam our mate because she or he spent too much of our hard-earned money.

It's frightening how destructive money can be to homo sapiens. What was that song the O'Jays sang in the 1970s—*For the*

Love of Money? They said for the love of money people would kill their own brothers and rob their own mothers. We see a litany on the news every night of sick stuff people have done for the almighty dollar. My father wrote a song for the LTG Exchange, his R&B group back in the 1970s, called *Money Mad*. Accompanied by a slamming beat and funky bass line, the song's lyrics focused on how everyone in our society—from politicians to morticians, teachers to preachers—had gone money mad. My dad just got a royalty check from Italy, so somebody must still be playing the song.

In a love relationship, serious money discussions are usually as welcome as a talk about what's wrong with our sex life. Couples will break up, marriages will crumble, longtime love connections will splinter in two over money issues—and the thing will end without the couple ever having sat down and had a heart-to-heart. In addition to being something we all want in as much abundance as we can manage, we are all incredibly defensive about our relationship with money. I know I read Denene's opening to this chapter while holding my breath, just waiting for her to dis my money management approach so that I could get all upset. It is truly the evolved and unique couple that can even broach the topic of household finances without somebody's feelings getting hurt and the discussion blowing up into World War III.

I watch my seven-year-old son, who is an extremely bright kid, but not able to grasp the concept of money and its importance, and I wonder how we lose our innocence. Give the boy a quarter and 15 minutes later he will have no idea what happened to it. But he'll be able to pinpoint the location of each of his action figures. Money has no meaning to him right now; he knows it's terribly important stuff, but he still has no use for it. So how do we go about transferring such extreme states of neuroses to our children when it comes to money? What magical words do we utter to them during childhood that turns money into the most important thing they will ever hold in their hands?

We could blame society or music videos or rap music, but I don't think these factors have nearly as much influence as our parents. If music videos were that important in our development, what we would dread with a passion later on is a discussion with our mates over how big the ice around our neck should be, not the dwindling checking account balance. My parents raised us with the attitude that money was important because it enabled you to eat and live the way you wanted to live, but it was not something to get all stressed out over. It was much more important to live life on your own terms and not be controlled by a job or even a career. Thus I'm much more laissez-faire about finances than my wife is. My attitude is that the money will be there when we need it; we don't let the worry about what will happen 12 months down the line stop us from doing something we want to do today. My wife does want to know exactly how much money will be in the bank 12 months down the line before she makes a move today—unless that move entails buying clothes or housewares, which aren't usually at the top of my must-buy priority list. (Though I'm finding it a lot harder to be upset at clothes purchases for my precious little girl than at another pair of Via Spiga pumps in my wife's closet.) These radically different approaches can cause some tense moments, and we've had our share. But what we must strive to keep in mind is that it is crucial for us to be respectful of the other person's outlook whenever we are having discussions or making decisions. We know there are differences and thus the possibility for conflict. We have to approach every discussion prepared to alter our approach enough to accomodate hers. This is a lot harder than it sounds because it means compromise, which doesn't come naturally to most of us. We need to meet somewhere in the middle: She'll buy fewer shoes if we work less overtime and spend more time at home; we'll cut down on the golf paraphernalia if she takes up her own hobby so she'll stop worrying about our hobby.

We are all so scared of money talk that *compromise* shouldn't be a hard word to remember. It'll eliminate a lot of sleepless nights.

If your man is contributing more money to the household than you, should he be able to spend more than you?

From a Sistah

Nice try, but I don't think so, baby cakes. The point here is that if it's the household's money, then no one person has more rights to it than the other. It's our money, honey.

I think that the way Nick and I handle our money is somewhat unorthodox. We decided when we moved in together years ago that I would have my own checking account, he would have his, and we would divvy up the household bills and pay them from our accounts.

It's worked for us.

When we were first married, we tried to do the joint account thing, in addition to our separate accounts. And while our separate accounts are fine, the joint account thing hasn't quite worked out. Sure, there's money in it on occasion, but because we are so used to having our individual accounts, the joint account really isn't a priority.

I don't think this is the way most households are run, though. I would venture to say that most couples, after they make the commitment to be together, combine the balances in those checkbooks and make joint decisions on how the pot is going to be spent. This,

I would imagine, is no easy feat; you have to be way more responsible with that bottom line when someone else is paying attention to it, too.

The key here, though, is the word *joint*. It means that the money from the two parties involved is joined together into a mutual pot, for mutual use. I don't think anyone is supposed to be keeping tabs on who put more into the account, and I certainly don't think the person who provided that extra cushion has more rights to the pot than the other.

See, I figure that if you two agreed to put your money together, then you spend it together. That means that you both make decisions on how it's spent, when it's spent, and the amount that's going to be spent. Now, I understand that this means that the poor, unfortunate woman who has a mate keeping tabs on the family spending would not be able to just stroll on into Bloomie's and pick up a pair of suede boots without conferring with her man—but it would only be fair. Same goes for Mr. Man and whatever money vice he has. No conference, no spend.

I bet you wouldn't be asking that question if she were making more money than he. The very thought of her making more money, and, therefore, earning more rights to the spending probably has a few brothers rushing for the porcelain god as they read this. There's no way in hell that sistah with the higher earnings would get to spend up more money than her man—no matter if she was pulling in attorney dough and he was only bringing in enough for cookie dough. Her decision to spend up the money she put into the joint account the way she saw fit would just K-I-L-L him. Pull down his pants and hold a knife to his jewels, why don't you? It would certainly hurt less than letting some woman tell him how their money is going to be spent.

Well, just as I'm sure you wouldn't take too kindly to your higher income–earning woman removing more of the funds from the account than you, we wouldn't take too kindly to our men doing this to us. The money, after all, is there for our mutual benefit—nothing more, nothing less.

I would argue that the way Nick and I handle our finances—or at least the way we fantasized it would be handled—would be best for many couples. You know, she has her account, he has his, they both agree to put some money into a joint account to pay the bills, the living essentials, et al. Whoever earns more money—whether man or woman—should put a higher percentage of income into the mutual pot, just to be fair. But that should not give that person any extra rights to the loot.

So when it comes time for her to buy her food processor? Or when it comes time for him to buy his ball machine to improve his tennis game? It comes out of their own personal accounts.

The rest of it needs to be left alone until both of you decide how it should be spent, keeping in mind that no one has more say than the other.

When do guys think it's appropriate to enjoy the money we've saved together? I mean, rainy days seem to come every other day, but we don't get to spend on those days, either. What's the deal?

From a Brother

Usually, if we're doing this right, the joint money is being accumulated for a reason: a new house, a new car, a new kitchen, a new patio, private school tuition for our little one, etc. These are big-ticket items that require careful planning. Unless we're just able to roll like that, we're unlikely to pull into the Lincoln-Mercury deal-

ership and leave in a new Navigator unless we've had some serious discussions and done some preparation beforehand.

If this joint money is used for less expensive things, I see all kinds of problems arising. You say the two wage earners will put money into the account without worrying about who is spending more of it, but what happens in real life is that both parties pay real strict attention to who gets to buy what and how often. That's just human nature—nurtured from the first time you went to the ice cream parlor and were old enough to notice that the sundae your sister traditionally ordered cost a whole lot more than your simple vanilla cone. You stop ordering cones, suddenly developing a jones for sundaes.

Whenever I've lived in a joint account household, I've paid strict attention to how much my partner was spending so that I'd know when I had a license to go out and buy something of my own. I knew instinctively that if I bought too many things in a row, she'd lodge a complaint. So if I wanted a new suit or a new tennis racquet—in other words, something I didn't really need—I'd wait until her non-essential purchases had reached such a critical mass that she wouldn't dare complain about my little suit. As a matter of fact, it was almost fun restraining myself from making purchases, wondering if she were starting to develop any guilt about her excessive spending. On the flip side, on a few occasions when I saw something I just had to have but had already made too many purchases in a row, I'd buy the thing anyway and just hide it somewhere until she had bought enough things to justify my purchase, at which point I would unveil it as though I had just picked it up that morning.

It's a strange feeling to get married or involved with someone seriously enough that your spending habits become fodder for family discussion. If we've been single and earning a decent living for a while—or, in this age when people are waiting longer and longer to get married, earning a decent living for at least a decade or maybe even two—how easy is it going to be to sit there while this other person asks what you could have been thinking when you paid $900 for a new exercise bike? How could you have been so insensitive as to buy something that expensive without checking with her first? My God, the nerve. And you're thinking, Damn, how did we get here? Is this what marriage is all about?

Allowing both partners to keep separate accounts might make the transition to a joint lifestyle a bit easier. A good friend of mine who grew up as an only child used to tell me that his wife always accused him of not being able to think like a couple. In the area of finances and everything else, she said he thought of himself first and foremost and was incapable of viewing the two of them as an inseparable unit. Well, this friend is now married to another woman and has been magically cured of this problem—raising the question of whether that was the real "problem" in the first place—but I think the hardest part about learning to live with someone else is figuring out what "thinking like a couple" means when it comes to finances. Do I have to call her on the cell phone if I want to stop off at Bloomie's and buy a new shirt? Will I get in trouble for getting my car detailed without putting it on the floor for family discussion first?

If we're going to make it as a couple, we have no choice but to figure these questions out, sooner rather than later. It's scary as hell and somebody is going to get their feelings hurt, but financial honesty is essential if you want your marriage to thrive.

Keeping Money Secrets

From a Sistah

My best girlfriend's nana is the one who put this in my head—and frankly, I thought it was brilliant.

"Always stash a little cash on the side, just in case, baby," Nana constantly schooled me and my girlfriends. "You never know where life will bounce you—make sure you're not bouncing broke."

Amen to that.

See, Nana's philosophy was that there are so many unexpected twists and turns in daily living—not to mention relationships—that any woman caught in the hailstorm of life (read: her man gets low on dough, or, even worse, he decides to up and leave her broke and lonely) best make sure she's got on her good walking shoes and a matching pocketbook filled with dollar bills y'all. After all, a woman has to remember her main interest in life: making sure she can feed herself and the babies, if there are any, just in case things don't work out.

Hey, it was a philosophy that worked quite well for Nana. She had worked as a maid all her life—on her knees, scrubbing and cleaning up after white folks, knuckles gnarled from years of the hardest labor any one person should have to endure. When she married, that didn't end; he was a day laborer who had to seek out work every day of the week from people who needed a hired hand around for short stints at a time, and, so, like a host of other African-American families from that era, it took two to make sure the six mouths in her household were going to stay fed.

And Nana and her husband loved each other hard and strong. They had four beautiful children together, and it was no easy task keeping a family of six clothed and fed in the 40s in the South, not with all the restrictions and racism and downright silliness that relegated black folks to second-class-citizen status.

Still, all that strong hard loving came to an end. Sounds like a cliché, but one day, Papa just up and left his wife and kids—no word, no warning. And Nana was left holding the bag. How was she going to feed those kids? Clothe them? Keep a roof over their heads? Provide them with life's basic necessities?

Thankfully, Nana—like a whole lot of women from her generation—had been tucking a few dollars she'd gotten here and there in a sock she kept in an old pocketbook at the bottom of the closet. Her decision to do this was not based upon low expectations for her husband; she was saving the money so that she'd be able to help her children get a leg up on life when they went to college or got married or what have you. She wanted to be able to hand over an envelope to each of them, and wish them a happy life, with love, from Mama.

And it's a good thing she did, because had she not saved up that money, she wouldn't have been able to meet the next month's rent after her husband left her, or buy the groceries for the next few months, or purchase those much-needed pairs of shoes for the kids for the start of the school year.

Years after her kids were grown and on their own, Nana was still putting money into that sock at the back of her closet, to the right of the new bedroom set she'd bought for her new condo in an exclusive neighborhood in upstate New York. That sock money, you see, had not only kept her and her kids clothed and fed through the hard times, but added up lovely for her when it came time for her to go on ahead and do something nice for herself. No, she didn't collect any interest over the years, but she sure didn't have to worry about bank fees—and once she put it in the sock, it didn't come out until it was absolutely, positively necessary.

To this day, two of Nana's daughters have socks in the backs of their closets, and another keeps stacks of savings bonds in a safe-deposit box intending to pass them along to her only daughter when she makes her mama proud and goes off to college.

I've never quite had the willpower to do such a thing; I just know my forehead would get hot and my palms would sweat knowing there was a wad of cash in my closet. I'd immediately find a reason to bring it with me to the mall—for those new suede Via Spiga boots I'd had my eyes on.

But I certainly admire those women who have the willpower and gumption to set aside money for a lonely rainy day. For when the kids need a helping hand. Or they want to treat themselves to something special. Or the man just ain't actin' right.

Still, I recognize that this is a problem for some men. I mean, I would probably have a problem knowing that my man was stashing money on the side without my knowledge, with intentions on doing something with it that might not include me. I mean, my husband's money is my money, and my money is his money—theoretically.

But then there's reality.

And sometimes, reality bites you square in the ass.

And you have to be able to afford the Band-Aid for the boo-boo.

That's where the sock would come in handy, dandy.

I know, however, that this is a serious problem for the men-folks. Perhaps you can explain:

Why do guys get all worked up when they find out we've stashed a little cash on the side?

From a Brother

Just like everything else in a relationship, money is based on a mutual trust—when we make some of it, we let the other person know about it. This doesn't necessarily entail accounting for every dime like your mate is the damn IRS, but when we're talking large stacks of cash, something is amiss if you feel like you need to hide it from me.

Growing up, I saw plenty of relationships in which the husband and wife kept money secrets from each other. From what I could tell, these were usually not the only kind of secrets being kept. The hidden money was just one symptom of a pairing with serious problems. Secret lovers, secret medical problems, secret trips, even secret families were all part of the program in these relationships. We're not talking about matches made in heaven here. They had so many secrets that you were led to wonder why they still bothered to call themselves a couple. I think after a while they got so used to hiding things that there was no point in ending the marriage—after all, divorce courts are notoriously intolerant of secret bank accounts and secret families. Rather than endure all that prying into their lives, it was probably a lot more convenient to just stay together in appearance but keep their secrets hidden.

This is not the kind of relationship that I want to be involved in. I want my partner and me to trust each other enough to share funds. I have heard many women say they have always been told to keep their own money on the side in case things go wrong in the relationship and they need to be self-sufficient. The fear and insecurity are understandable, but there seems to be an underlying assumption that the man to whom you've pledged your everlasting love will be the future source of your fears. He's the thing from which you might one day need protection. How am I supposed to feel about that but lousy? Something tells me this kind of thinking isn't uncommon, particularly among black women. Brothers had been made into such ogres throughout the 20th century that our women have grown up thinking they need protection from us. Imagine what that does to a little girl's psyche, to go through her formative years with thoughts like that rattling around in her head—"You gotta protect yourself from these men out here, even after you find one and fall in love with him. You need to have your own cash that he doesn't know anything about."

Ouch. That hurts my feelings.

You hear that often enough, and as soon as you meet the man of your dreams, a part of you is going to wonder how long it will take him to try to hurt you. As you gaze lovingly into his eyes you will have a hand behind your back tucking away the twenties as quickly as possible. The two of you happily start planning a future together and what you're thinking at the same time is when he finally does pick up and jet, you'll have $5,000 in that secret account to keep you going. This is not the best foundation on which to build long-lasting devotion. We will talk a little later about prenuptial agreements, which women almost universally despise, but your thinking in these money cases sounds suspiciously like the male pre-nup argument for which you show major contempt. If I can't do rainy day planning when I'm worth $2 million, why is it okay for you to do it with your little $2,500 you've been diligently tucking away? Your rainy day planning is even more despicable if you know I've been struggling to keep that roof over our heads and you've been sitting over in the corner with your stash, not saying a damn thing. That's dishonest and destructive. If I find out about it, I'm going to be pissed. So then you're trapped because there's no smooth way for you to find an extra $3,000 or $4,000 when we need it without me being suspicious about its origins. Oh, you got an unexpected bonus? What was it for, honey, seeing that it's the middle of August and last month you were afraid you were about to get fired? Did anybody else in your department get one? No—just you? Wow, you must have worked really hard this month, which is curious since you spent three weeks of it on vacation.

Not sounding very smooth, is it?

You know what I start doing when I suspect you're holding out on me? I start stashing some cash myself. So where does that leave us, two people supposedly in love taking portions of their hard-earned dollars and hiding them from each other in a game of secretive one-upmanship? We start looking silly and suspicious and untrusting, and eventually that's the way we start acting toward each other. I think you're hiding money from me because you're planning on going somewhere. And no telling what you're thinking if you find out I'm hiding money from you. You probably start crafting all kinds of doomsday scenarios in your mind—like other women and children I'm supporting across the Northeast. Ugh! It's making me feel creepy and slimy just writing about it.

Now none of this is to say that we shouldn't have separate checking or savings accounts, or that I should know the exact balance in your account down to the numbers behind the decimal point. That level of surveillance isn't necessary. We're talking here about the big-ticket savings amounts—monies exceeding $1,000. You got an extra $200 you're keeping on the side so you can jump on that next one-day sale at Macy's? I understand and won't quibble with that kind of planning—because I'm going to be doing the same thing myself. You dip every once in a while into your 401(k), penalties and tax consequences be damned, to buy a new coat or to make sure you have extra spending money for that vacation we've been planning? Not a thing wrong with that, my sistah. But if you're putting $100 from every paycheck into a money market account I've never been told about, with the idea being that you want to be prepared for the day when I'm no longer around, then something is wrong. You're worried about what will happen to you upon my demise? We'll take out a life insurance policy and make sure the family is taken care of in the event that I perish. That's what life insurance is for. You can even keep the policy in your own little folder, amongst the other files that are crammed into your whack filing system in that overburdened corner of the nightstand.

If your needs are taken care of and I'm not trying to hide my cash from you, do you still need to monitor every entry in my checkbook ledger?

From a Sistah

Yes, because it's my money, too—and damn if I won't be privy to every penny that comes into this household. Shoot, somebody's got to know how to spend it.

See, what kills me is that you all readily argue that our money socks aren't welcome in the closet we share—that saving up money on the side for a rainy day is not only counterproductive but downright sacrilegious. But here you are asking me why I need to know about every dime you have.

Well, let me hip you to my reasons:

1. I may run out of money and need some of yours. You will not be able to tell me you don't have any to give me.
2. I may have money but be reluctant to spend all of it, so I'll need some of yours. You will not be able to tell me you don't have any to give me.
3. You may decide that you want to leave, and then try to argue in court that you really don't have all that much cash for child support and alimony. Say it with me: You will not be able to tell me you don't have any to give me.

It's this simple—no more, no less.

Really, I don't need to know about every dime, darling. The small change in your pocket? Keep that to yourself. But I would be a fool not to know about the checking account, the two savings accounts, the money market, the 401(K) plan, the life insurance policy, the trust fund, the three business accounts, and the envelope behind the second drawer in the etagere off the foyer.

Spend about 10 minutes in divorce court, and you will understand why.

The world is full of men who spend the entire marriage making all kinds of money—sometimes with the wife's help, sometimes at her and the kids' expense—and then, just when things get really good to them, they decide to run off with the young(er) chippy with the long legs, the video ho looks, and the personality of a frozen Pathmark pea. And damn if they don't try to take all the money with them, so that they can lavish expensive baubles and trinkets on their new little playthings.

Meanwhile, the kids need college tuition, school clothes, books, winter coats. And mama needs a new pair of shoes. And yes, you should be paying for them because, in part, it is because of me that you have anything anyway.

I'm just making sure that I get what's coming to me.

But it is impossible to do that when we aren't privy to all the info.

Hate to bring up yet another *Waiting to Exhale* reference, but damn if Terry McMillan didn't cover all the bases in her landmark book. Remember what happened to Bernadine when her husband asked her for a divorce? He left her up in that expensive house, alone with two kids and no disposable income to pay for the mortgage or the living expenses—and then tried to offer her a pittance of what he was worth to get out of the marriage. Bernadine didn't take it; instead, homegirl hired a smart sistah-girl lawyer, who found all the money he'd made from the company she'd helped him set up—some of it in his mama's name, some of it tied up in businesses she didn't know about, more of it in places she wouldn't have dreamed existed.

It took a smart lawyer and a tough-as-nails divorce court judge to give Bernadine what she rightfully had coming to her.

Yes, this was a book—but I hardly think it's unrealistic. The newspapers and gossip columns are even more saucy, with multi-millionaire athletes and businessmen doing to women what they wouldn't do to a dog: leaving them in the cold, with no money, to fend for themselves. A dog, though, can get picked up by the local animal control officer and get put out of its misery.

But not her. She has to figure out how to pay those bills, keep those kids fed, keep that house up—and the only way she can possibly do that is to get her rightful share of your money.

Now, she won't have to worry about all of this if she has an honest man sharing her bed.

An honest man does not hide his money and assets. Indeed, one has to be wary of the man who would be so damn cheap and secretive with his money that he would go out of his way to keep it from his family. That's the kind of man who isn't honest—the one who would hold on to a dollar tighter than a crackhead does a glass dick, then lie like a rug when someone, including his wife and children, asks him for something they truly needed, never mind simply wanted.

No need to tell you what that man—if you want to call him that—would do to his own wife in a divorce court.

I suppose you would look at this differently, though.

Why do guys try to hide the amount and sources of their income?

From a Brother

I don't think anybody, including my wife, should need to know at all times exactly how much money I've got in the bank down to the penny. Giving another person that kind of intimacy with my cash just makes me nervous. Maybe it's just force of habit. If I round it off to the nearest hundred, is that enough information for you? And as for the source, I don't have a problem telling you where my bread is getting buttered—unless of course I'm keeping that information away from you to protect your safety (this is for the brothers who roll on the illicit side of the ledger on occasion. I'm trying to put something in here for everyone, even y'all crooked behinds).

What happens is this: We get used to our money being our own business. The whole world is nervous about revealing too much information about their money to anybody else. Unless you're really tight with someone, they'll look at you as if you're wacky if you ever ask even the most innocuous questions about their personal finances. Go ask a co-worker how much they paid for their car, or how much their mortgage is, or how much they pay their babysitter. Watch their eyes widen; watch them squirm. It's considered rude and unseemly to request information like that, so over the years we get used to people not asking us for details about our finances. It even feels strange when our accountant throws all those money questions at us. I'm not sure where this comes from. It's certainly not there when we're little boys and girls. No one is less circumspect with money than a little kid. They'll pull out every dollar and cent they possess and proudly show it to strangers passing by on the street. Of course, ten minutes later they won't even remember where they put the money. As teenagers, we're still not all that private. We don't hesitate to tell someone how much we make at our after-school job or how much we paid for our new leather jacket. Oh, we'll be ecstatic about sharing the cost of our clothes with anyone who cares enough to listen. Things don't really change much in college. We don't have any money in college anyway, so there's nothing to talk about—except when we're begging our homey to let us borrow some so we can get a slice of pizza at two in the morning.

But then we walk onto the floor of our first job, the hotshot young college graduate eager to kick some ass. Every person in the joint has their eye on us. Some are jealous; some are suspicious; some are attracted; some are annoyed. What is the one thing every single one of them is thinking—besides wondering where in the world we got that butt-ugly tie?

How much is he making?

We know they all want to know but we also know they'll never know. Over time a few might make some lame attempts to get the information out of us, but we will easily rebuff their half-hearted efforts. Our salary, our money, is our own damn business. We plan on keeping it that way.

A few months later, that pretty woman in accounting starts spending a lot more time in our department, lingering near our desk when she clearly doesn't need to be. We are flattered and quite attracted. We ask her out and before we can say "back that thing up," the two of us are a hot item. Weeks turn into months and she is finally ready to pop the question: "How much do you make?" She asks it casually, like she doesn't really care all that much. But we know she's poised on the edge of her seat. For a split second it crosses our mind that once we let it out of the bag, it could conceivably make its way back to our nosy co-workers who have been dying to know. But this is our girl, and we're eager to impress her, so we give her a figure that's close enough so we couldn't be called a liar if she ever found a pay stub, but that still has a little padding in it to make us look as good as possible.

It will be years before she'll get any information more specific than our approximate salary. Maybe when the two of us move in together and we have to start making large purchases, she'll find out about savings accounts and investments and anything else we might have. But details will be sketchy at best, primarily because she knows how it feels when another person is quizzing her on exact numbers. She knows how badly it will make her look, how it'll make us start wondering about her intentions. Is she going to gank us for our little bit of bank? What's up with the questions, the detail? Just imagine how it would look if we caught her up in our checkbook, scanning for the balance. It'd look suspicious and shady as hell. We'd start wondering if we could even trust her alone with our stuff. Well, it's kinda that way when she's asking all kinds of questions, too. Most people just don't do that, even our wives. I'm in my second marriage now, and never can I recall my spouse asking me for the balance in my checkbook.

So, what is my point? Simply that we don't necessarily go out of our way to hide our income—we're just not going to go out of our way to share every detail. Before we met our women, we got used to the privacy of our accounts, the knowledge that no one knew how much money we had but us. We have a hard time giving up that privacy. It doesn't even mean we don't trust our women. It just means that the sanctity of our intimacy with our cash is gone, shattered, when we have to start reporting on the bottom line to another person. Of course that's what a marriage or a serious relationship is all about, but we don't always give that up so easily. It will give us pause, make us nervous. Eventually you will find out what you need to know, but don't be offended if the information has a hard time falling from our lips.

As for the sources of our income, we're likely not as guarded about this information. Even if we get money from many different sources, which most of us don't, it does us no harm to divulge these sources. That doesn't mean we're telling you how much we make—we're just telling you where it's coming from. If I have a newspaper job that pays me a salary, I teach in a writing program on the weekends, and I write freelance magazine articles on the side, I'll tell you this without hesitation. I'll even be proud to let my woman know how enterprising I am. But if you start asking how much, don't be surprised if a cat wanders by and steals my tongue.

Food, Fun, and Incidentals: Does He Always Have to Pay?

From a Sistah

Nick gets on me every time for this, but this girl just can't help it: Whenever we leave the house together, I almost always—at least 70 percent of the time—leave home without the three necessities: money, keys, and identification.

Well, maybe 80 percent of the time.

Okay—always.

For the life of me, I just can't explain why. I mean, I was raised to always, always have money in my pocket, in case of emergencies, and especially if I didn't want some negro thinking I owed him something because he paid and I didn't. And I spent more than a little bit of time sitting on the stoop after school, waiting for someone—anyone—to come home and let me in the door because my house key would, undoubtedly, be anywhere but in my bookbag—a continuous goof that forced me to learn to make sure I had my keys somewhere on my person before I slammed the door shut. And Lord knows black folks been pulled over by the cops enough times that we should all know better by now than to *think* about leaving the house without some form of I.D., unless we really just want to spend some time behind bars on some trumped-up "you're in jail because you're black, dummy" charges.

Certainly, there was a time when I followed all of those rules. Wouldn't catch me leaving the house without I.D.—too scared of the idea of some big chick named Bertha making me her girlfriend. (That, and my dad telling both me and my brother that if we ever found ourselves behind bars, we better not call him, because he would deny we were his and we would just sit there forever, becoming more and more emaciated from eating nothing but bread and water until the day came that we wilted away to absolutely nothing and quite literally rotted behind bars.) And while I'd gotten locked out of my apartment a few times, having realized after it was too late that I didn't have my keys, I usually remembered to bring them with me when I went out.

And you could bet your last dollar that I had some kind of money in my pocket, or at least an ATM card so that I could hit up my checking account if I ran out of hard cash—particularly before dates. Had to offer to pay my way, or I just wasn't going to eat or be entertained. That was just my way.

Then I got hitched.

Actually, I got a steady boyfriend.

And all of that stuff just flew out of the window.

My guess is it's because I just grew to expect that Nick would have my back like that. I mean, he almost always drove when we started dating (I was living in Brooklyn, and, therefore, smartly carless) and *always* drove after we started living together (except for the time when I told him to slow down because I wanted to arrive alive, and he got mad and made me drive everywhere for, like, two months), so it only made sense that it wouldn't be a big deal if I didn't have my keys. If he was always driving, he'd always have his keys, right? So I didn't need mine.

Ditto for identification. If I wasn't driving, there was no need for my driver's license. And if I wasn't carrying my driver's license, then I didn't have to carry my wallet, which made me happy, because if I wasn't carrying my wallet, then I didn't have to carry my purse—something I've always hated to do. What I'd mostly end up doing was slipping a $20 bill in my pocket, just in case—the just in case being just in case Nick wasn't paying.

Nick always paid, even when I offered to pay myself.

He's a gentleman like that.

So after a while, I stopped worrying about bringing money with me, too.

And that easy, I was walking out of the house without my keys, my identification, and my money.

There are plenty more women who do this, too, much to men's chagrin.

And while you guys happily skip along with this in the beginning of the relationship, at some point, you all start huffing and puffing if we get somewhere and, all out of the blue, when the bill comes, you look at us with that "Ain't you payin'?" look all up in your face.

And, of course, we're all confused because you've been paying and driving all this time, and now you acting like we're wrong for not offering like we used to.

Why do you guys pay for everything and drive everywhere when we first start dating, then flip the script and act like we're greedy, insensitive, forgetful boobs when, after we've been dating for a while, we leave our wallets and keys at home?

From a Brother

We don't have a grand plan to one day become stingy after the relationship has been chugging along for a while. That's not it at all. What we have over time is a slowly eroding checking account.

It's easy to pay in the beginning—we know it's what's expected of us and, as long as we got the cash, we figure that the angels in heaven will smile down kindly on us for our gentlemanly generosity. Some of y'all may even give us a little sumthin' sumthin' every once in a while as a token of your appreciation. Those tokens act as positive reinforcement, making it easy to pull out the wallet the next time. Yeah, I know you're going to say that you'd never sleep with a guy just because he paid for your dinner, but sometimes we can't help but make a connection between the two (particularly if we're going for all the gusto and splurging at some ritzy joint that we know Takisha wouldn't be peeking the inside of unless she was applying for a job). To be honest, it actually feels kinda good to open up the wallet and be able to pay for a fancy meal. It makes us feel like a big shot, like a man who has accomplished something with his life and doesn't mind letting others bask in his well-founded bigheartedness. Naturally, there are always going to be some of us who take this too far and foolishly throw cash around like a new lottery winner, trying to make Master P look cheap by comparison. Those brothers are a pox on the rest of us, but there's nothing we can do about them but laugh behind their backs.

Eventually, though, the relationship settles into a nice, comfortable rhythm. We stop feeling like we have anything to prove, particularly to our woman. And as we get to know her better, we make another discovery: Homegirl brings home just as much cash as we do—or maybe even more. Contrary to the oft-expressed views of the female population, this fact doesn't necessarily mean we will go

40

up to the roof and leap to an inglorious death from our embarrass-ment. Most of us are capable of accepting her higher salary and moving on. Maybe even bragging to our friends about how accom-plished she is—yes, ladies, we have been known to do that, too. But the next time we are out to dinner together—or maybe just buying some damn ice cream cones at Carvel—her salary is going to start blinking before our eyes like a big gaudy neon sign as we pull out the wallet. We will pry the wallet open and take out a few bills, all the time stealing glances over at our lady, who is all smiling and giddy from the sugar rush of the tiramisu or strawberry Carvel cone. Reaching into her cavernous pocketbook to fish out some crum-pled-up twenties is the last thing on her mind. In fact, she might not even be carrying the cavernous bag with the money in it—more likely, she'll have one of those cute little numbers that's maybe large enough to hold a pack of Tic Tacs. When we see her stroll out the door with that little mini imitation of a pocketbook, we know our wallet will be losing some weight tonight.

This will go on for some time—years even—before we would dare mention anything to her. First of all, we really don't know how to mention it without sounding like a cheap bastard. So we make really lame little comments every once in a while, like, "Uh, where's your wallet, dear? I, uh, don't have any more singles." Of course, you'll smile brightly and say, "Oh, that's okay, honey. I'm sure they can give you change."

If things get real bad, we might even go so far as to purposely leave our wallet home one day. The point would be to teach you a lesson, but naturally the real lesson will be learned by us—don't leave your wallet home, stupid—as we try to explain to the waiter why we have to rush out to a cash machine to pay for the meal.

The peculiar thing to us is how our women allow this to go on for years and years without having a problem with the imbalance and unfairness of it. We will be cohabitating in a relationship in which all expenses are supposed to be split down the middle—we might even sit down with a calculator and divide up the bills down to the last penny—but all this meticulous planning is blithely forgotten by our women whenever we walk out our front door together. We become the Public Bank, required to pick up all expenses whenever we're in public. We may not lose a lot of sleep over this particular problem, but it does bother us, particularly when the checking account is dangerously low and we've just made fancy dinner plans for the weekend.

The fact that you often leave the house without money proves that you expect a man to always have money, doesn't it?

From a Sistah

Sure. Why wouldn't we? Weren't we raised to expect nothing less than a man who would pay?

Look, my offering to pay my own way is quite a revolutionary concept, one that I talked about in a chapter in my book *The Sistahs' Rules*. Again, it's something that my father drilled into me from the time I could understand the words that were coming out of his mouth: Always have money in your pocket so that you can pay your own way—that way, the negro won't expect anything from you. It was sound advice, and I turned it into a very good habit.

But can I tell you how many sistahs had a problem with that rule? I mean, my telling them to pay their own way—or at least offer to pay for dinner every once in a while—was just a concept that was completely unheard of. "What? Offer to pay? Shoot—if a man can't pay for my dinner, then he's not worth keeping, with his cheap ass," they'd say.

Over and over and over again.

And I could understand why. We were all raised to believe that a man bears certain responsibilities in a relationship, and chief among them is that he do the courting, and we be the courted. That means that he pursues us; we either accept or decline the offer. He makes the dating plans; we go along with them. He pays for the meal, or the museum or the theater tickets; we thank him for the lovely evening. He tries to get into the apartment after shelling out said money for meal, museum, and theater tickets; we don't let his ass in until at least after the third date.

Period.

And you all got the same lessons, too. Don't get amnesia.

So why, then, in the new millennium, would you think we wouldn't expect you to not only have money in your pocket, but to pull it out when it comes time to pay for the things from which we'll both benefit—like dinner, or entertainment, or even groceries, for that matter? Was there a new rule book that was handed out to the brothers to which we sistahs are not privy? Did someone hold a convention and proclaim that men are no longer responsible for being, well, men?

Quite obviously, I'm not into that feminist bull that demands I forgo being treated like a lady because anything else would make me less of a woman. To hell with all that. In my mind, there are some very clear lines that should be drawn when it comes to male/female responsibilities. No, this does not mean that I'm against women's rights, I fully expect to receive equal pay for work equal to that done by my male counterpart; I fully expect that I won't get treated any differently from a man in any place of business, club, or social venue; and I fully expect to pay the same amount as any man for any services rendered to me. That means that I shouldn't be getting less money than my male co-worker who isn't nearly as good and who doesn't have as much experience as me. That means that I best be able to get into the same country club as my husband, for the same amount of money and with the same privileges. That means that all those foul dry cleaners are wrong for charging me $3 to clean my shirt, when they charge Nick only 99 cents to launder his, even when it's damn near the same exact one as mine—only bigger.

But there are just some things men are supposed to handle.

Like, you're supposed to open the door for me.

You're supposed to offer me your seat on a crowded train.

You're supposed to offer your hand to me to help me step out of the car, after you've opened the car door for me.

You're supposed to take the garbage out.

You're supposed to wash the dishes if I cook.

You're supposed to drive.

You're supposed to go outside and start the car so that the passenger seat can be warm.

You're supposed to carry the heavy bags.

You're supposed to get the oil checked in the car.

You're supposed to know how to plunger the stopped-up toilet—or at least know the phone number of someone who can.

You get the idea.

Surely, in the year 2000, single women with no man to assume those responsibilities learn to do it on their own. Lord knows I did all the years that I lived by myself. A woman should know how to be self-sufficient, just as a man should know how to do the things they've always deemed women's work, like laundry, or cooking, or changing diapers.

But there are women out there who think "Damn if I'm hauling some garbage to the curb when I have a man to do it." Likewise, there are some women who think "Damn if I'm going to pay for dinner if he's taking me out."

I don't necessarily agree with the latter, but I can understand. **Didn't we all get the same lessons when we were younger— i.e., men ask women out, then pay for the date and everything else that comes up?**

From a Brother

It's not the first few dates or even the first few months of dating that's the problem. The problem arises when the expectation goes on for years, deep into a settled, long-standing relationship. A relationship where the two partners have painstakingly figured out how to divide everything up to avoid just the kind of pique that I'm describing now. Yeah, I wash the dishes after you cook, that's dividing up the responsibility. But where's the fairness in me paying for every one of our meals and everything else when we're out for the rest of our lives if you bring home a nice fat paycheck just like me?

Not only is it illogical to me that you expect us to keep paying, it sounds like y'all just want the Get Over. You ask me about whether the rules got changed when you weren't looking—well, I ask you, were any men in the damn room when we came up with this rule in the first place? It made sense at a time when the males were generally the breadwinners and the women were expected to stay home and tend to house and family, but we all know that's not the way it usually works anymore. Now it appears that you all want to have your cake and eat it too, literally. Equal pay for equal work and all that, but we're crazy if we expect you to pay for the vittles every once in a while.

I guess I can't fault the females. If things had worked out differently and we were in a situation where society had dictated that males would have their meals paid for into infinity, we'd also be fighting hard to preserve the Get Over. We'd be telling anyone who would listen that things have always been done that way, dammit, that it's tradition and all that, so why we gotta go and change up the program now? We'd lay out all the ways in which we are deserving of that extra concession and we'd say we still deserve it—even if we are killing ourselves to be treated equally in every other area of our lives.

And do you really want to get into how most of us—male and female—were raised? If we went by that standard, y'all would be paying for your own dinner and damn near everything else too, 'cause that's what many of us saw in our households—particularly in the African-American community. Our papas don't exactly have a real strong history in this regard. And even if we did grow up in a household where the man was paying for everything when he and his wife went out to dinner, no one ever really sits us down and explains it to us. My mother and father never told me that my woman would expect me to pay for everything for the rest of my life. I had to learn this one on my own, after a whole lot of awkward moments in my early years when I was scared to death that I didn't have enough money for the entire meal. Remember college? We were lucky if we reached the weekend with two dimes to rub together, but if we got up the nerve to ask a woman out on a date, our broke ass had to find enough cash to pay for it—though she knew we were broke. It might have seemed a little strange or unfair to us, but soon we just accepted this as the natural order of things. However, little did we realize that it continued straight through marriage, even if we had one of those modern marriages in which everything is shared, and what recently formed couple in the new millennium doesn't have one of those?

The Get Over is alive and well in the new millennium because y'all continue to fight for it. One day we might look up and see a contingent from the National Organization of Women on the steps of the Capitol Building, carrying picket signs and getting that good shout going—some lyrical message like "Hey Hey Ho Ho, Women Shouldn't Pay for Stuff No Mo'."

Help Wanted: What Happens When He's Out of Work?

From a Sistah

Okay, maybe it's just me, but I see them everywhere: HELP WANTED signs. At ShopRite, at Pathmark. McDonald's, Burger King, and Pudgie's. Home Depot and Pier 1 Imports. My local pharmacy. Kids R Us. Toys R Us. Babies R Us. My dad told me you don't even have to speak English to be hired at Entenmann's bakery, where he worked for years. And when I went to the local Rite Aid near my parents' house to get some film developed, the woman handling my order told me that in one week, she'd worked over 40 hours in this, her part-time, decent-paying, no-experience-needed gig, and she and her co-worker had actually started taking turns babysitting each other's kids so that they could cover the hours that would have otherwise been occupied by a third worker.

And, like Robert Townsend's grandmama said in his film *Hollywood Shuffle,* "Shit, there's always jobs at the post office."

So what's the problem? Why, pray tell, are there 850 bazillion brothers standing on the street corners, sitting on stoops, and chillin' in front of the liquor stores and bodegas, with their hands in their pockets, like they don't have jack bone else to do? Why are those same brothers pushing our children off the neighborhood playgrounds and basketball courts in the middle of the damn day, like these safe havens were built for them and not for the kids? Why, can we ask, has almost every brother to grace the stages of Ricki Lake, Jenny Jones, Sally Jessy Raphael, Montel Williams, and Jerry Springer gotten up there on national television and acted like it was his God-given duty to not have a job and to freeload off the big sister with the *really* big heart but absolutely no sense and no game?

Just asking—because, you know, it's not like there aren't any jobs out there.

Oh, wait—I can hear it now, the international brother moan (stretch out hands on either side, shrug shoulders, cock head to left, bend knees slightly, narrow eyelids, lower bass in voice several octaves): "Why I gotta work at ShopRite? I'm waitin' for a good job."

Uh—like a $60,000 gig at Microsoft, with stock options, bonuses, and incentives is going to come knocking on his door talkin' 'bout, "Open up—it's me, Job. Any brothers around with no education, no résumé, no job experience, and no wardrobe? Got a spot for ya."

Don't get it twisted: I'm not suggesting that every black man out there is a trifling, unemployed, basketball-bouncing-in-the-middle-of-the-day, nothing-but-jeans-and-sneakers having, ain't-half-looking-for-a-job, uneducable, lazy ass. I know good men—grew up at the knee of the hardest-working man outside of show business (Daddy), admired the son of that hard-working man, who is equally hard-working and more dollar-wise than most folks (Troy, my brother), strove to be like the ever-independent, do-it-yourself man who quit The Man's job to start his own successful law firm (my brother-in-law, James), and married a man who has the qualities of each of them (Nick). But for every black man who is doing it and doing it well, I would venture to say that there is another one making the KKK extremely happy, as those men—if you want to call them that—are proving time and time again that the stereotypes white racists have of black folks aren't fallacies in all too many cases.

Why do men pass up perfectly good jobs, then sit around blaming their dire straits on everyone but themselves?

From a Brother

Ouch. Don't hold anything back, babe.

I've heard every reason ever concocted to explain the plight of the black man in the United States—the vestigial effects of slavery and its destructive influence on the black man's sense of family and his motivation to toil for the white man; the methodical emasculation that this country has engaged in over the past century to break down the black man; the discomfort white employers have with placing a black male in their midst; the feelings of sexual inadequacy of the white man and his absorption and belief in every black male sexual stereotype; the desire of the white man to keep his prized, pedestal-perching white woman away from the black sexual he-man. But I still must admit to many of the same thoughts as you when I see the brothers on the corners in the middle of the afternoon. Their presence has become so common that most of us would probably sense that something was wrong if we drove into a decaying urban neighborhood and didn't see any brothers standing around.

Of course, the problem with the excuses I listed above is that, though there may be truthful elements to them all, you can find hundreds and thousands of brothers who overcame them and circumstances much worse to get that good job, to remain faithful to that loving woman and make her their wife, to support that family, to do the right thing. It's an argument I've heard in education circles many times before—if you can find one school full of poor kids who are excelling, then all kids should be able to. If thousands of black men can succeed against the odds, then they all should be able to.

But that's just not the way our society was designed.

Surely I've also grown tired of the brothers who blame their plight on this racist, capitalist economy, but there's much truth in that argument. I'm not an economist, but it's pretty easy to see that there are just not enough high-paying, desirable jobs in this country to accommodate all the people who want them. The education system isn't well funded enough to give sufficient resources to everybody who needs them. The college and university system isn't vast enough to educate all the people who could benefit from a good education. In other words, this thing is set up so that many of us will fail. That's the flip side to the Ronald Reagan, Booker T. Washington, up-by-the-bootstraps, Horatio Alger fable that we like to parade in front of our children. Sure, if you work hard and single-mindedly go after what you want, you too can become Puff Daddy. But the odds are overwhelming that you won't make it. I bet if you go down to that corner and talk to the brothers, quite a few are waiting for the Puff Daddy break. And they will keep waiting until some misfortune finds them and they become another statistic.

According to the U.S. Census Bureau, there has been a 24 percent rise in this country in the working poor over the last few years. The working poor are those people who have jobs but don't make enough money to lift their families above the poverty line. Many of them have the kinds of jobs you listed above—the Toys R Us, Pathmark, Burger King–type jobs. They work hard at those jobs, yet they are still poor. When I was covering poverty issues for *New York Newsday*, I grew to understand the predicament of welfare mothers who had made a conscious decision to reject the dead-end, low-paying jobs being offered to them and instead spend the time raising their kids. Of course, society has nothing but contempt for their decision, but it was quite rational and understandable.

First of all, you don't know how many of the brothers on the corner tried the Rite Aid or McDonald's jobs in their pasts and concluded that they would be better off hustling on the street for the next dime. I guess it's more respectable to put on that polyester uniform and report for burger-flipping duty every day alongside the high school juniors and the senior citizens, but lots of brothers eventually got fed up with that menial existence and opted out. And without that good-paying job, it's pretty hard for all that other stuff to fall into place—solid relationships, marriage, supporting your children. Can you imagine the despair that must overcome these brothers when they wake up one day and realize that they're 32 years old with no high school diploma, no marketable skills, no real place to call home, no knowledge of where their children are and what they're doing, and no future to speak of?

Faced with those circumstances, most people would just go back to sleep.

In other words, no matter how much we wish otherwise, there's always going to be the brother on the corner in the middle of the afternoon. That is the hand that our community has been dealt.

How long can I be up in your house without a job before you start questioning my manhood?

From a Sistah

Now, I don't know about all the other sistahs, but I can firmly tell you this: I come from the Gwen Guthrie school of "No romance without finance," which basically means that an unemployed brother in the Millner household would get exactly two minutes of my time—one to tell me he ain't working, the other to get the hell out of my house.

Homey don't play that.

I guess that's just how I was raised.

Don't mistake my thinking, fellas, for that of a gold-digging bitch; I am neither a money-grubbing pigeon, nor a really mean female dog. I'll tell you what I am, though—and that's James and Bettye Millner's daughter, and any daughter of James and Bettye Millner knows that she best have a man who can take care of business, lest the daughter and her man be called out as trifling asses by said parties.

Let me give you some background: My father, a native Virginian, has worked nearly all his life—literally. When his mother died, he was but 11 years old—old enough in those days to quit school and work to help the family keep food on the table. There were no help wanted signs in those days; Daddy worked for his daddy, who owned a wood service in Danville. But had Granddaddy not had his business, my father would have done anything—lawns, construction, farming, anything—to keep himself, his dad, and his six siblings fed.

That mentality didn't end when he left home at age 16. Daddy has had so many jobs in his lifetime, I can hardly keep up with them: sweater maker, chef, worker in a plastics factory, and bakery foreman are just the few I can recall him talking about. Each kept money in his pocket—kept him alive.

And though we were hardly rich, my father always found a way to give my brother and me what we needed, and even what we wanted. He was—and still is—the best kind of man, a provider who makes sure his family is taken care of. It's how men in his day were taught to be—no trifling negroes from 'round his way.

To his credit, Daddy taught me to be the same way, but he wanted me to be even smarter; he wanted his daughter to set her sights on a trade and go to college, so that she could be the most independent woman she could be. I always had my own job, always had my own money, always paid my own bills. No, I wasn't—and still am not—perfect; Daddy helped me out a lot with my luxuries. But he wanted to make sure that his little girl got what she could on her own, and whatever else she wanted that she couldn't afford was going to be gotten by one man and one man only—her daddy.

That meant that I was not to depend on some man to give me the things that I wanted and deserved. I either had to get it on my own, or ask him for help. Period.

But damn if Daddy was going to let me get with a man who wasn't *capable* of giving me what I want. Of course, he wanted his baby girl to marry a man for love—a man who had only the best intentions for his well-deserving daughter. But Daddy fully expected me to pick a man who could be financially stable and had the means to take care of his family, like a real man should. Any man who couldn't handle his business in the money department—well, he simply wasn't a man.

If he wasn't a man, he wasn't to be with James Millner's daughter.

I like that rule. A lot. For most of my life, it has kept me out of the middle of a whole lot of dumb shit.

Now, even though my father grew up in the South before integration and the Civil Rights Movement and affirmative action and job opportunities for black folk, not once have I ever heard him suggest that some white man kept him from working. You'd figure that a black man who survived the KKK, segregation, Jim Crow, and the worst kind of racism any racial minority could face would have a whole lot of madness to blame on white folk, and justifiably so. But Daddy just didn't do that.

Which is probably why I'm not trying to hear that "The Man" is keeping the black man down. My motto? Can you help me pay my bills? Can you help me pay my automobile? Can you help me pay my telephone bill? Then maybe we can chill.

This doesn't mean that I haven't allowed myself to be used. Hey, I'm human, and it happens to the best of us. No, Denene is not perfect, and my hard head did make for a soft behind on several occasions when it came to giving some dumb, lazy negro the benefit of the doubt.

The one that got over was this brother I dated up in Albany—a barber by trade, except he never really had a chair anywhere. "They want too much of your money around here," he said of the supposedly onerous rents barbershop owners wanted to charge him for the right to do business in their buildings. He'd sit on his stoop all day, spinning conspiracy theories about how "The Man" stopped him from going down to the mall and filling out that application at The Gap. And there I was, working hard every day, paying my bills, hardly surviving, hours away from my family and friends, listening to this grown man trying to explain why he didn't have two pennies to rub together and his rent was due. I didn't make a whole lot then—saw more than a few days where I ate peanut butter and jelly sandwiches because I couldn't afford anything else. But my rent was always on time, even if I had to go without a few luxuries (like a bed, which I didn't have until a year after I moved out on my own).

Still, I found myself more than a few times spending my hard-earned money on groceries for two. I found myself constantly filling up my gas tank so that I could take him where he wanted to go. I found myself constantly pulling out of my wallet twice the amount of money I should have at the movie theater and at the bowling alley.

I found myself getting played.

This is why he is an ex.

Been there.

Done that.

Got the hell out of Dodge and so glad that I did, because had I stuck around, I probably would have still been slaving away while he took up all his time sitting around, talking about how "The Man" was forcing him to sit on his ass all day.

Now, there are some men who would readily argue that black women should stick by their men, and should understand that it's hard for the brothers out there and that the last thing they need is for a sistah to devalue the devastation racism has wreaked on the male psyche and his ability to take care of his financial responsibilities. I can firmly say that I know racism exists; I get blindsided by it at least once every other day and twice a day on the weekends. But I also know that most people with sense can find their way around it, and that real men can walk through it if it means that their family is going to be taken care of.

My father did it.

My brother did it.

My husband did it.

Real black men do it. For the sake of their women. And their babies. And, above all else, themselves.

Because, after all, he's not a man if he can't put food on the table and reasonably take care of himself and his family. I honestly don't believe this way of thinking is that of a gold digger or a heartless sistah who doesn't respect or honor black men. It is the thinking of a woman who believes the impossible, because she's lived with the impossible.

Still, there are neighborhoods full of black men who continue to make the excuses while they lay up in black women's homes, taking advantage of their desperate, natural need for companionship. And they don't seem bothered by it one bit—no matter how many times their lot shows up on Ricki Lake. So, question:

Do men ever get embarrassed about being out of work?

From a Brother

Hell yeah. Even I sometimes get embarrassed that I don't put on a suit and go to work every day—and I make a damn good living sitting home at the computer and writing all day. This idea of an honest day's work is a peculiar thing, nurtured by our fables about the strong, hard-working "real" men of our past. Many of us have been bred to believe that if the work doesn't entail sweat, dirty fingernails, and a lot of grunting, then it's not real work. It's soft. And the person doing it isn't a real man.

What's ironic about this is that many of us were raised by parents who dragged their behinds to an ungratifying, non-skilled job every day with one thought in the backs of their heads: I am doing this so I can send my kid to a good college and he/she can sit in a big office behind a big desk one day. But that same kid grew up watching Mom or Dad toil away every day at the non-skilled job, and a part of him feels a little guilty that his workday might end without him breaking a sweat or lifting anything heavier than the phone receiver. Or that kid gets married to a woman who watched her mom and dad toil away every day, and a part of her feels like her man isn't as much of a rock-solid real man as her father was because he sits behind a desk every day.

This tortured thinking has come up in my relationship with Denene on occasion because she often tells the story of her father and his hard work when we're speaking before audiences. She'll say that her father always taught her to check a man's hands to see if they're hard and calloused before she got serious about him because that way she could tell whether he's hard-working or not. I always took immediate offense at this because the only calluses I got on my hands are from gripping a tennis racket. They are clearly not the same caliber of callus Mr. Millner was talking about. But that doesn't mean I haven't worked hard over the years to support my family and won't continue to work hard in the future.

I grew up watching my father engaged in artistic pursuits: He was a musician who spent long hours at the piano writing songs and composing music for his 1970s R&B band. It was fascinating to watch and it definitely had an effect on my decision to become a writer. In addition, my parents ran a record shop—at one point they had two of them—so they were their own bosses, working hard to support the family on their own terms. This also had a profound impact on me. I grew up thinking that two of the coolest things in the world were to sit down and create something that you could share with the world, that might even move other people, and to work for yourself on your own terms. To me, that was real manhood, and real womanhood, too. I guess it's no accident that I now make a living as a writer. The idea of physical labor never really crossed my mind in my formative years. Sure, I saw my dad do things around the house that needed to be done, but if there were any directions or clues that I got from him and my mom about my future, they were centered around me going to a great college and doing great things in the world. When I was a young, gangly pre-adolescent, my mother used to tell me that she had a feeling that I was going to be famous one day. That's some heady stuff for a little boy, but powerful at the same time. Talk about high expectations—hers were so high that when I was slaving away at newspapers early in my career, achieving a small amount of noto-riety among local readers, I once asked her if that's what she'd meant by my future fame. She tried at first to squirm out of an an-swer, but soon it became quite clear that her answer was "No." Being a successful newspaper reporter wasn't it—that wasn't the kind of fame of which she was speaking. So I knew I couldn't stop there if I was going to fulfill my mother's destiny for me. I had to go on and write books, which explained why I would wake up three hours before I had to leave for the newspaper in the early days of my career, pounding away at the keyboard writing novels that no one likely ever will see. I had a sense that if I kept writing them, one day I would write one that was good enough to be pub-lished. I suspected this was the kind of fame she had in mind.

That's all to say that when I came across my wife's definition of a hard-working man, passed on to her by her dad—a wonderful man whom I respect immensely and who has much to do with the fact that my lovely wife is such a sensitive, warm, and loving mate—I resisted. This picture of manhood as defined by physical toil didn't fit into the images of manliness that I grew up with. In fact, it never even crossed my mind that this is the way much of the world defines manhood until after I graduated from Yale and entered the real world, one in which most people spend most of their energy pushing themselves to make it through the day up in some white man's workplace so that they can run home and get some sleep and do it all over again. Deep thoughts, intellectual pursuits, creativity are the furthest thing from most people's radar screens—unless it's finding a few hours before you doze off to absorb the results of someone else's creative endeavors on television or radio. On a few occasions after college, I had women touch my hands and notice their softness and make some laughing, derisive comment about the lack of hard work in my past. These comments were understandably bothersome and would come rushing back to me when Denene went into her speech about hard-working black men and what her father taught her. I couldn't help feeling like she was making some kind of comment on the quality of my manhood, that I wasn't quite the man her father was or that she was told to go out there and find. Usually when I'd interject during her monologue she'd contend that I shouldn't take her and her story so literally—that a man who works behind a desk to support his family can work just as hard as a man who does physical labor. I'd partially believe her, but I'd always wonder why she insisted on repeating over and over again in city after city the part about the calluses.

All this stuff came rushing to a radical head when I decided to leave the newspaper business and write full-time at home. Once it became clear to us that it was financially feasible, I still wondered if I would be even less of a real man if I didn't leave for an office when I woke up in the morning. The life of a writer is a peculiar one. So much of your work goes on in your head that you might be toiling away in earnest while driving to the store for groceries, or running around the park. Not even other writers—including your wife—know when you're working because it's an invisible labor. So if you have any insecurities about whether others think you goof off all day, it's hard to shake them when you do much of your work upstairs.

These fears are quadrupled for black men because we carry around so much baggage about what the world—and our women—think of us. So many other black men who walk around in sweats in the middle of the afternoon might not be up to anything at all, so why would I appear any different to anyone who glanced my way? Black men necessarily spend so much of their time reacting to what others will think—sometimes not even consciously—that it impacts many of the decisions we make during the day, from the path we will walk to the store to the shoes we will wear. I know that the reason I cared so much about the clothes I wore when I went to the newspaper every day was because I wanted to make sure people knew I had a good job and earned a good living. Others would call me a clothes horse and marvel at a man who seemed so interested in clothes, but what they didn't know was that the clothes were my protection. It becomes clear that this is the origin of the stereotype that so many black men really *do* seem more interested in fine clothes than men of other racial groups. My clothes immediately signaled to the world that I wasn't like those brothers you see standing around on the corner. I was different. I wasn't trifling. I had a job.

But at the moment I don't really have a job. I write books. I don't get to wear my expensive suits until I go to book signings or on book tour. What do people think about me? Yeah, I may be the most relaxed and stress-free and happy I've ever been in my adult life, but am I still a "real" man? I don't have any calluses; I wear sneakers in the afternoon; I go jogging or play tennis. Am I being lazy? Is this lifestyle too easy—shouldn't I be more tired at the end of the day if I were really toiling away to support my family?

As you can see, the perceptions of others about our job status are terribly important—even if we're not prepared to admit this to the world. Why do you think so many brothers find it necessary to spin these tales about "The Man" and how cruelly this society has treated them? They are trying to tell anyone who will listen that there's a good reason for their current sorry state—that it wasn't just their own doing.

6

Pre-Nups

From a Sistah

S he did love him—had for what seemed a lifetime. Their partnership was a great fit, it seemed—he was a professional basketball player, she a practicing pediatrician. His offering her his hand in marriage was really just a formality, seeing as they'd dated for six years after catching each other's eye at a glitzy who's who party in New York, and that they'd fallen madly, hopelessly, helplessly, immediately in love.

Or so she thought.

Exactly one week before they were to wed in a spectacular Maryland ceremony, ol' boy sat her down and presented her with a pen and a document thicker than one of those black and white composition notebooks. She was to sign the pre-nup, no questions asked, no lip-service given. Just sign it.

Well, to her credit, girlfriend had sense enough to read it before it even hit the table—and sense enough to get the hell out of Dodge before they both made a huge mistake and she woke up in prison, charged with stabbing his cheap, dumb ass. Why? The pre-nup was insane. He'd set it up in such a way that he'd have total power to micromanage their love, their marriage, their future family, and her life—down to how much weight she was allowed to gain during the course of their partnership together.

Yup, she had to maintain the 125-pound Coke-bottle figure she'd chiseled out on her 5'8" frame, make sure to leave her shoulder-length hair the same, and "maintain the standard of beauty" he'd grown accustomed to in the six years that they'd gotten to know each other.

Boyfriend—one of the NBA's top-dollar ballers—also wanted her to bear for him three children, no more, no less, go back to work after no longer than nine months of maternity leave, and agree that she wouldn't ask for one red cent over an allotted household stipend during the marriage and not a dime in child support in the event that things didn't work out and they divorced.

And that was in, like, the first five pages, y'all.

None of us could believe the nerve, no, outright audacity, of this guy—that he would actually stoop so low as to tell a woman how many children she was going to bear, but that she had no right to seek support for those children, and that she would have to maintain her 30-year-old figure after pushing out those three babies for him—even into old age.

Needless to say, the minister, the caterer, the hall, and some 250 guests got a free Saturday out of the deal, because girlfriend wasn't even thinking about marrying his ass.

And why would she?

He'd demonstrated that six years of commitment, honesty, companionship, and love meant nothing once they exchanged vows and rings—that he didn't trust her enough to even fix her hair right, let alone be a good wife, loving mother, and hard worker after they said, "I do." He'd also shined the light on what kind of husband, father, and lover he would be by outright saying that he—a multimillionaire—had no intention of taking care of his children in the event that the marriage didn't work.

No, he wasn't the one for her, at all.

Still, he would argue to this day that she was a gold-digging tramp who showed her true colors when she refused to sign a pre-nuptial agreement that he felt protected his bank account, tastes, and heart.

Tell the story to a brother, and he will swear up and down that the baller knew exactly what he was doing. In the midst of a raging debate over the pre-nup at my job, all the men said that her refusal to sign it was indication enough that she was just after his money.

"If she really loved him, honey wouldn't have had a problem with it," one of my co-workers said.

"She probably couldn't wait to get to his money," said another.

"Forget all y'all cheap bastards—ya low expectation–having mofos," I shot back.

It wasn't even worth discussing, because it was clear that the men and the women were on two totally different sides of the issue and there was no middle ground to be seen.

Help us out here:

Why are pre-nups so important to men?

From a Brother

Well, for most of us they aren't that important because we don't have the kind of loot that we need a team of lawyers to help us protect anyway. But the idea behind them is both simple and beautiful: If she's trying to hitch a ride to my money train, she needs to show me that her intent in entering into the relationship isn't to stick me for all my papers.

I would imagine that a single man (or, in many cases, a married man) who has amassed a prodigious sum of money becomes quite attractive to the opposite sex. In fact, I don't even have to do much imagining to understand that—all I have to do is wash my car to get a few inquiring looks from women on the street. A shiny car is enough to signal to them that I'm deserving of a close look. If you happen to be a prominent and easily identifiable rich guy—for instance, if you're seven feet tall and your picture regularly stares back from magazine covers, or if your video is in the once-every-10-minutes rotation on MTV—you might as well have a big target painted on your back because the women will run you down like lionesses swooping in on a poor defenseless antelope. Besides discretion and home training, what defenses do you have against a grinning and luscious lady hypnotized by your cash? Yeah, you can say no and tell her to leave you alone, but what if she comes off as sincere, smart, sophisticated, and sexy? You might find yourself become a little entranced by her. Next thing you know—*bam!* She done smacked you upside the head with her 38 DDs and grabbed all your hard-earned loot.

But then there's the pre-nup. As far as defenses go, the pre-nup is the goal line stand in the final seconds of the game. It's your last chance to emerge from the game with a W. Without it, she rolls right over you like a tank all the way to the bank.

Washington Post reporter Kevin Merida wrote a compelling 1998 series in which he followed 18-year-old NBA rookie Tracy McGrady, who had jumped to the Toronto Raptors directly from high school. McGrady had received so many warnings about the dangers of treacherous groupies that he sometimes literally ran away from attractive women who approached him, according to Merida's stories. The NBA runs a Rookie Transition Program in the summer that includes discussion of pre-nups and gold diggers. It's not only expected but commonsensical that these players would find ways to protect their newfound wealth.

For every case like the NBA knucklehead you mentioned above, who went so far with his pre-nup that he may have placed a permanent taint on a lovely legal concept, there's an Anna Nicole Smith. The wildly blonde and zaftig Smith made a name for herself a few years back when she threw her gigantic globes up in the face of the rich old Texas billionaire J. Howard Marshall (who was more than three times her age) and, when he came up for air—no doubt reaching for the oxygen mask—she was elbow-deep in his hard-earned stash of cash. Years after Marshall's death, the courts awarded Smith half of his estate—about $500 million. I can understand how Marshall would become intoxicated by Smith's (mostly) natural gifts, but what I don't understand is how he could have fooled himself into thinking homegirl was after anything but his cash. Did he think this blonde nuclear warhead (bombshell is too tame) had fallen for his charm and 89-year-old good looks?

I would think that women would welcome a pre-nup after falling in love with a rich man. After all, by signing on the dotted line, she has an opportunity to allay his fears and prove that she loves him for him, not his money. Otherwise, he's going to have his nagging suspicions eating away at him at the first sign that she has fallen madly in love with his cash. And the idea behind the pre-nup certainly isn't to leave the woman broke if the relationship does crumble. That would be cruel. We just don't feel that she should get half of what we have if she wasn't around when we accumulated it, and she had nothing to do with the accumulation. Seems like common sense to me.

For average brothers like myself, we dream about being in situations where we might need to have a woman sign a pre-nup, but most of us bring so little into a marriage that it never even crosses our minds. We know our ladies are unlikely to come after our *Sports Illustrated* collection or baseball cards if the relationship ever comes crashing to the ground. Pre-nups are something we'll only read—and dream—about.

If you're not a gold digger, then you shouldn't have a problem with pre-nups, right?

From a Sistah

Negro, please. A sistah is always going to have a problem with a pre-nup, because inherent in that stack of paperwork is the fact that the man you love thinks that you are eventually going to stick him for his papers. If he's thinking that she's going to gank him, then that means he doesn't trust her—and, if she thinks she's not trusted, then the basis for their relationship is built on one big, fat, hairy lie.

Isn't trust, after all, what a marriage is supposed to be built on? Don't the vows say, "For better or for worse, for richer or for poorer, in sickness and in health?" That means that these two people have vowed before God and their mamas that they're going to stick together, *no matter what*, and no man is going to put asunder what they've built together.

All of that becomes null and void when he pulls out that pre-nup, because with it, he demonstrates that he doesn't think the marriage is going to even last, let alone that his woman can be trusted. With each page and every letter on those pages, he says to his woman that he thinks she has the potential to be a thief—someone who will rob him blind (demand a high sum of support) if given the opportunity (a divorce).

He is also saying that he doesn't respect her or their union enough to allow her to reap the rewards sowed during the marriage. When two people decide to marry, their property becomes community property, the family being that community. When Nick and I decided to live together, my couch became his couch, his stereo became my stereo, our towels became each other's towels. I got the keys to his ride, and he got the keys to mine because they are *our* cars now. And as for our money—we've pretty much built our bank accounts together, so who would he be to tell me I could only have a certain percentage of the money that I helped him get?

Even if I didn't work outside the home, who would he be to tell me that I wasn't putting in hours of hard work and earning a fair share of the money he made during the course of the marriage? Shoot, if I'm home with the kids, making sure dinner is on the table, his drawers are washed, his toilets are clean, his friends and colleagues are entertained and that he is happy, happy, joy, joy during the majority of our relationship, you damn skippy I want my piece of the post-nuptial pie, because I would have maintained his life and his household in such a way that enabled him to make mo' money, mo' money, mo' money. Exhibit A: Viacom chief Sumner Redstone and Phyllis Redstone, his wife of 51 years. No, she didn't work. But she was there for him for that entire 51 years—was a dutiful wife who cooked, cleaned, and helped him become the media king of the world by making homelife a heck of a lot easier than it could have been if he was there by himself.

And how does he repay her? He goes out and finds a young, blond Hollywood producer chippy to keep him warm when he's away from home. How does Phyllis repay him? She demands half of his estimated $60 billion, and gets it.

And she deserves every cent of it because, by God, she stood by her man and earned her keep for over five decades. Do not tell me that a stale piece of paper with an order that she get only, say, $1 million of his some $60 billion after 51 years of marriage is remotely fair.

Every woman out there knows that she put in *work*, okay? Nothing upsets us more than when a man proclaims that *he* was the one who made the money, and, therefore, *he* should be the one who gets it all, no matter how much work *she* put in. Simply put, it's about the *we,* darling, and that doesn't stop just because we're talking about the benjamins, what?

Now granted, there are the gold diggers out there who will rob yo mama blind if you don't keep an eye on them. But then, if you know she's a gold digger, what the hell are you doing putting a ring on her finger? Seems to me that you would have sense enough to know that this woman isn't the one you want to marry because she's interested in your money, not you. Exhibit B: Donald Trump and Marla Maples. Need I say more?

By the same token, neither I nor any woman I know would want to be with a man who would pull out a pre-nuptial agreement that would essentially state that, no matter how long we are together and no matter how much I assist him in turning his thousands into millions, or millions into billions, I am not worthy of sharing in the windfall if things don't work out between us. A prenup would essentially tell us that we should lay down, shut up, and die without reaping the rewards of our labor.

Basically, we think it fair that the courts decide. Shoot—that's what they're there for, to make sure that the money and assets are divided in a fair and equitable way. Now, granted, the laws can be a bit tilted in our favor, I will admit—but the extra money and support we're receiving is almost always due to the fact that we are the ones taking care of the children.

What I would say is if a marriage doesn't work out and you guys don't want to get stuck for your papers, get a good lawyer and fight. Don't pull out a pre-nup before the relationship even starts, as we will take it as a sign that it is doomed.

Wouldn't you?

How would you feel if I slapped you with a pre-nup days before we were to get married?

From a Brother

And what exactly are you trying to keep my hands away from, your shoe collection? Just hand me that pre-nup and tell me where to sign; if we reach the point where I don't want you anymore, I surely don't want any of your stuff.

Brothers who enter into relationships with women who are paid walk around under such a thick, viscous cloud of suspicion that most would likely dive for a pen to sign that pre-nup and prove that they aren't interested in her money. If you doubt this cloud of suspicion, think back on all the mean things you've ever heard said about Stedman Graham, or Larry Fortensky (one of Liz Taylor's exes), or Tom Arnold, or any other man who has made news by attaching himself to a rich and powerful woman. If you're truly honest, you might admit to having said a few choice words yourself. The rest of the male population takes note of these comments and whispers a silent vow: If I ever get lucky enough to fall in love with a rich and powerful woman, I'm going to make sure everyone knows I am not trying to grab her money.

As I've said before, the male population considers it lame to lure a rich woman into a relationship just because she's rich. If we want to be paid, we won't feel right about ourselves unless we go out there and make our own money. To let her do all the work and sit back and reap the benefits—or get paid because of her rich blood—has a stench of wimpiness to it. We can't go out like that. We derive our sense of self from how we look, what we do, and who we're with. That middle one probably reigns supreme over the other two. If I'm a neurosurgeon but I'm also butt-ugly, I will probably get enough attention and adulation from enough people to compensate for those unsightly thoughts that race through my head when I look in the mirror. As a matter of fact, I'm probably going to try to avoid mirrors—they will do nothing for me but ruin my day. And as for who I'm with, Mr. Neurosurgeon isn't likely to have many problems in that category either, even if he's cracked a few mirrors in his day.

If we're going to be in the practice of employing pre-nups, I think they should be deployed well in advance of the wedding day. It would be a little too tacky and insulting to whip the document out during the rehearsal dinner and watch your future life partner crumble into a thousand little pieces. You have to bring this stuff up earlier in the relationship, before you are even sure that the thing is going to lead to long-term commitment. It might even be a good way to gauge the depths of the other person's interest in you—rather than your money. If I casually mention over cocktails a few months into the relationship that I will require any woman I marry to sign a pre-nup, then my girlfriend doesn't have to take it so personally when I produce the document a year later. She knew it was coming and she has no real case if she's trying to quarrel with me over it. I've established up front that this is my general policy. If you don't like it, you can get to steppin' right now before this gets too serious. Pull the papers out the day before the wedding and it's going to look like you gazed at your mate and saw GOLD DIGGER stamped on his/her forehead, causing you to dive for the phone and call a panicked meeting with your attorneys.

I can understand how all this pre-nup talk could be distasteful to some guys who are afraid of offending their potential life partners. We're aware that this topic creates such hostility in most women that you all start having Lorena Bobbitt fantasies if you hear the word "pre-nup" fall from our lips. For many guys, the potential of the pre-nup to explode a perfectly fine relationship into a thousand little nasty pieces is enough to stay away from the subject altogether. But the rest of us will look at the pre-nup like life insurance—certainly it's not the most pleasant of topics, 'cause we want to live forever, but we still gotta have it.

Part II

Power

Does Money Equal Power?

From a Sistah

Ladies, take your pick: Money and no man, or his money and The Ring. Because you can hardly ever have it both ways.

Money, you see, equals power. It gets you the best seat in the restaurant, gets you into the best section of that pricey neighborhood, gives you the chance to court the influential—convinces people that they need to drop what they're doing and kiss your ass.

Makes you Big Willie.

Everybody knows that only boys have willies.

And the bigger men think their willies are, the more they'll stick out their chests.

They get louder.

Become all-powerful.

Unsinkable.

Immovable.

Real Men.

Let a woman get some money and a little power and most men will think—and in some cases treat her—like she's about to chop off their willies.

She becomes the bitch.

She becomes the butch.

She becomes the uncontrollable man-hater.

She becomes the emasculator.

She becomes the loneliest sistah on earth.

Because no man wants to cede the kind of power that comes with big money to a woman, lest he not be bothered by the fact that his manhood will be questioned on the regular. Sometimes, even, by himself.

Rather than deal with said questions, he will simply move on to a woman with less money. Less power. Less issues to address. Someone who will not try to tell him how the money should be spent, where it should be spent, whom he should spend it with, and the amount that should be spent.

And for all too many of us independent, speaking-up, climbing-to-the-top sistahs, what it will come down to is this: We will either have to give up the power or give up the man.

I've surely gone through it.

I actually lost a good man—or at least I thought him to be one—when I chose to take my career by the reins and decide my own destiny, without his input. I was a young reporter with the Associated Press at the time, and was being courted by a big New York City newspaper that wanted to pay me big money to do for them what I had always wished to do: cover politics in one of the most political cities in the country. The catch was that I would likely be a bit player in the scheme of things, rather than continue to be a much more respected and revered reporter at the small capitol bureau for which I was employed. My money was right there. My position was tight there. My power was neverending, because I got to do what I wanted to do. I chose to stay where I was. And he left.

I'd argue that a big part of the reason he didn't want to deal with me anymore was because I wouldn't take his advice and come back to New York City. As if he knew anything about my profession and what would make for a sound career decision.

Not.

I used my power to decide my own fate, and in the process lost my man, see? Of course, there are a few men who don't mind their women having money or power—but I think even a lot of them are more comfortable thinking we are truly too weak and daft to know what to do with either one. He may act like he actually wants some input from her, but the bottom line is that ultimately, when it comes to financial moves, he wants it to either be his decision exclusively, or he wants to pretend to care about her views so that later on, after he makes the decision exclusively, he can convince her that he actually considered her input. Very few of us are blessed with that special man who is comfortable enough in his manhood to exist in a world where his woman is powerful and paid.

So answer me this:

If I make more money than you, would it ever be possible for me to make the majority of the financial decisions in this relationship?

From a Brother

If it becomes clear to both of us that you are much better than we are at making financial decisions, then I'd like to think that we'd cede the authority to you in this arena. It wouldn't be because you make more money than us; it would be because we wouldn't want to go broke or have every creditor in town following us home from work because we weren't paying any of the bills on time and we

*were putting our money in all the wrong places. I will admit, how-
ever, that many of us might have a hard time getting to the place
where we could admit that we were screwing up our finances and
needed to hand over control to you.*

There are two stereotypes that will hover over our heads and
make this whole subject as touchy as can be. The first is that
women aren't as good at handling money as men. The second is
that black men aren't very good at handling money at all. So both
of us will be carrying major complexes with us into the breach;
both of us will feel we have something to prove and a vested interest in not making any concessions or admissions. If I see you
coming toward me with your hand out, asking for control over our
financial matters, I'm going to need to know that you aren't looking at me as just another Trifling Negro who doesn't know how to
handle his money. This may sound silly to you, but think about all
the images that bombard us featuring black men with huge
amounts of money doing very stupid things with it. Think about all
the pro athletes and entertainers who have amassed huge fortunes,
collecting expensive cars and phat cribs like most people collect
debts, and then wound up in *Jet* five years later talking about they
broke. Think about MC Hammer and Mike Tyson and Lawrence
Taylor and all the other knuckleheads who made big headlines
when their money dried up. Another black man becoming a laughingstock for wasting his money. It's so bad that beer companies
even make commercials mocking the phenomenon. Miller Lite
featured a black man supposedly signing a ridiculously huge con-
tract to play basketball, than offering a reporter a million dollars at
the press conference for his Miller Lite. I never thought that commercial was funny; it capitalized on the public's expectation that
black men with money will waste the cash in a heartbeat with their

silly knuckleheaded ways. These images have an effect on every hard-working brother out there trying to make ends meet. They give us even more resolve to be sensible with the little bit of money we have—and we pledge to be even more sensible if we ever strike it rich. And speaking of striking it rich, how many black men have we heard about who win the lottery and somehow manage to squander all the money? In the New York area, there was the heavyset brother with the bowler hat, Curtis Sharp, who was prominently featured in television commercials in the 1980s for winning millions. I read a story not long ago about Curtis having nothing left except a big pile of debt.

We never want to feel like we are being placed in the same category as the Curtis Sharps and MC Hammers. That makes it hard for us to admit you should be the one making the financial decisions. Once again, we are worried about what people—in this case, our lady—will think. Are we being put into the Trifling Negro box again? Does everyone realize that I'm just too busy and too distracted with more important things to concentrate on matters as mundane as household finances? That sound I'm hearing in the corner of my mind, that faint whisper of "Hammertime, hammertime, hammertime . . . "—where the hell is it coming from?

All this time, as we're concocting these conspiracy theories in our heads, you're thinking only that you are more diligent and know a little bit more about investment portfolios. The fact that we're of the same species as MC Hammer and Curtis Sharp of course never occurs to you—why should it? But still we fret.

As for the ladies, I'm sure many of you may interpret our resistance to handing over the financial reins as our assumption that you will mess everything up because you're a woman. That thought may never have crossed our mind—we may be too pre-

occupied with what you think of us to even consider any stereotypes we might have about women and finances. So there we are,
in effect both needlessly spinning our wheels because of stereotypes that are the furthest thing from our partner's mind. It sounds
silly, but these are the kinds of impasses that plague our relationships on a daily basis—assumptions, stereotypes, insecurities, and
complexes follow us around like our shadow. The only way we get
past them is to acknowledge them, grapple with them together,
laugh about them, and move on. But how many of us are in love relationships in which we can laugh about money matters? I would
guess not many. Money matters seem to bring together all our psy-
chological and emotional baggage into one big sour package that
always threatens to rot everything it touches.

If we are ceding control of financial issues over to our women,
the logistics become important—and delicate. If we started out
making the financial decisions in the relationship and we have
proven that we aren't fit for the job, there's already likely to be
some anger brewing on both sides. Our woman probably already
has quizzed us so many times about this or that financial matter
that we can't even hear her clear her throat when finances are on
the table without getting all pissed off and defensive. And if we
have been screwing things up, she will probably already be upset
at us anyway, making it even less likely that she will be able to bring
the kind of warmth and understanding to her tone of voice that we
might need in order to talk about this without throwing up our defensive walls. If the relationship is just beginning and we haven't
yet demonstrated we don't know what we're doing, there's a danger that we might take her statement that she should do the finances as a clue that she has put us in the Trifling Negro box. So
even if we don't want to be in charge of the finances, we might take

umbrage at her assumption that she's the best person for the job. Whew! I'm getting a headache just thinking about this stuff. Everything in a relationship has the potential for conflict, but I think matters like these have to go to the top of the list. Both parties have to be so aware of this potential at the start, otherwise the whole discussion will degenerate before the first check ever gets written. Reassurances, comforting, understanding have to be passed back and forth at every opening to keep the discussion as cordial as possible. But these discussions have to be undertaken, as unpleasant as they may be. It's when things are assumed or allowed to fester for too long that couples have the kind of fights that blow up and leave the relationship in a thousand little shards.

If it's primarily my money that's responsible for a major purchase, like a new house, should I have more say in the final choice?

From a Sistah

Uh, no. If my signature is going to be on the mortgage papers—and I know they would be because you ain't nowhere near that paid to buy a house by yourself—then I damn sure better have had equal say picking that bad boy.

I can't think of one single instance in which I would readily cede my input in major purchases with Nick just because he made more money than me. I mean, dang—it's hard enough being at the bottom of the totem pole in pay, in titles, in society as an African-American woman without having to deal with that mess at home.

Say we were going to buy a new furniture set for our home. Ideally, this is how it should work: We decide together what look we're going for, what brands would accomplish this look, what stores would sell those brands, and which stores would give us the biggest bang for our buck. Then we'd set up a mutual time when we would be able to go down and check out the goods—and the set that *we* agreed upon would be the one that *we* would buy. Your extra $5 shouldn't give you the right to pick out the hideous purple polka-dot couch and a 1,000-inch-screen television any more than my extra $5 would give me the right to decorate the entire bathroom with pink-and yellow-ribboned wallpaper and matching towels.

Like Al Jarreau said, we're in this love together—and no matter how much more one makes than the other, this is a partnership, and in a partnership, all is equal. Partners don't tell each other what to do; they either agree on the next move, or readily surrender their right to participate in the decision-making. The latter cannot happen with arm-twisting; that partner has to simply say, "You know what? Why don't you decide for us."

This is how it worked in my parents' house. When it came to big-ticket items, Mommy and Daddy always made the decision together. The house? They both decided to move back to New York from New Jersey back in the late '70s, and they both decided that Long Island would be a great place to raise children. They picked the house together. They decorated the house together, down to the color of the carpet and the pattern of the wallpaper. And they bought their cars together.

Sure, there were decisions that fell more on one shoulder than the other—as in any relationship. My dad surely never gave his input on what kind of pots to buy for the kitchen. My mother surely never told my father which lawnmower to buy. They pretty much had some passions that remained just that—their passions—and their mates knew better than to exercise any kind of rights over them.

But the main point here is that my dad readily accepted that just because he made more money than my mom didn't give him the right to make all the major decisions solo. I'm pretty sure that his motivation here was purely selfish: Daddy probably sought her help in picking out the big-ticket items because he didn't feel like hearing my mom's mouth if she didn't like what he'd decided on.

This should be every man's motivation.

The only time that a woman should not have any input in the purchasing of items like a home or a car or, like, a wedding ring, is when the man is surprising his girl. And even then, perhaps it's not that smart. What if she doesn't like the house? You mean to tell me that you would rather move your significant other into a house she may not like, just because you had more cash than she did and, therefore, had more of an opportunity to make the decision on where the two of you would reside for the rest of your lives? Or what ring she would wear? Or what car she would drive?

Some chicks may go for this.

I wouldn't.

You'd pay for it for the next 20 years. Maybe even 21.

Meanwhile, perhaps you can tell me this:

Why do men get so flustered about every little money matter in a relationship?

From a Brother

That's a question I've often wondered myself when I've noticed how my neck hairs were standing on end, my palms were dripping sweat, and my heart rate was doing a Carl Lewis impersonation just because I knew I was about to have a discussion with my mate concerning money. It's almost like we hear the word money *and our body releases some stress-inducing hormone that drives our nervous system onto the*

Autobahn, where it hits 120 mph in seconds. I think what underlies it all is fear. After all, the symptoms I just listed sound like a dead-on description of a person who is scared out of his wits.

What are we afraid of?

Money is literally the bottom-line indicator of our entire lives' worth as individuals, our value to the planet and the community, the quality of the life we lived. We can't help but think that a man who dies rich led a more complete, successful life than a man who dies poor. The rich man might have been a miserable old geezer who had long ago alienated his family and had to buy any comfort or love he could find—I was going to say he died alone, but I think rich men rarely die alone, even if they are despised by everyone around them, because hovering over everyone's heads is always that damn will and testament. The poor man might have been loved by everyone who came into contact with him because he touched souls. But still we can't help but use money as a measurement in our quick and easy evaluation of the lives they lived.

Men know that they are being judged every waking moment by the outside world based on how much money they have managed to accumulate. Sure, we pay lip service to the value of happiness and quality of life, but how many of us wouldn't want to change places with Bill Gates even if we were told that he was lonely and miserable?

Deep down, men are afraid of these money conversations with our women because we think one of them might result in our beloved turning to us, pointing an accusatory finger, and saying, "You know what, mister man? You are trifling. You have failed as a man because we don't have enough money."

We spend years in school, we study hard, we come out and toil long hours, all with the single-minded idea that we have to accumulate a certain amount to show that we have done it, we have conquered this adult thing. As we go through the years, we're always wondering whether we have gotten there yet, whether we are at the point where the world is going to look at us and say we have lived a successful life. A money talk with our woman puts all of that on the line, places us in imminent danger of this woman—and you sistahs know y'all can be harshly frank—breaking us back to square one by declaring that she is unhappy with our level of accumulation. Those are words no man wants to hear; in effect, it is the motivating factor behind much of what we do in our lives. We are trying to prevent our woman from concluding that we—in other words, she—doesn't have enough stuff, doesn't live in a nice enough house or apartment, doesn't have the ability to buy nice enough clothes or nice enough toys for the kids, doesn't have enough.

The awful thing about our women accusing us of being failed, trifling negroes is that once the accusation comes, there's little we can do to change it, reverse it, dismiss it. It's there, stuck on us forever like a scarlet letter, plaguing us during every waking day. In some cases this may give us a push to go out there and kick down some more doors, but most of us have already been trying to kick down as many doors as we can. We have already been toiling away in fear of being labeled exactly the thing she just called us. So when the label comes, many of us hang our heads in defeat. It becomes the defining moment in our lives, whether we want to admit it or not. Some of us may even give up, leave home, desert our families, embark on a search for the perfect bottle of alcohol or the most magnificent crack pipe.

Does this all sound overly dramatic to you? Are you starting to raise your eyebrows, like you are reading the ramblings of a crazy man? If you are nodding your head, then you must be a woman and you just don't understand. Because for us, there's nothing that puts it all out there on the line like a money talk with our mate. It is a circumstance fraught with all the dangers of an IRS audit. But while he may be frightening, the IRS man doesn't have the ability to make us sweep our gaze over the totality of our lives, to make us question everything that we've done since we snatched that high school diploma. The IRS man can't get us to ponder the meaning of our existence. But a money talk with our woman can. Some of us would rather be in the hands of the IRS.

8

Chores and Child-Rearing: Can They Ever Be Equally Divided?

From a Sistah

For this lady, it was really quite simple: Just fix the damn sink.

She didn't want to tell him, she didn't want to get a pen and pad and spell it out for him, she wasn't about to hire an airplane and have it written in the sky for the guy. She just wanted him to fix the damn sink.

And I felt her—this woman who showed up to a relationships panel we conducted at a black writers' conference a few years back. She'd asked a male panelist why men had to be told to do every little thing around the house, rather than take it upon themselves to simply do what needed to be done—and the ladies in the conference center went wild. We could all relate—understood how a woman could get vexed by a man who could walk past an increasingly disgusting pile of dirty dishes and never once think to wash them, or let a smelly garbage stink up the entire house without once considering to empty the offending can, or, in this poor lady's case, let the sink continue to leak without at least offering to fix it.

"I told him that my sink was leaking," she said simply, sternly, her arms folded across her chest. She described herself as a sixty-something, single, independent divorcée, and it was really quite obvious that this woman was no-nonsense. "The sink had been leaking for weeks. And you know what he said? He told me that if I went to Home Depot, he would give me a list of things that I'd need to fix it, and that he would show me how to do it."

Yeah.

She wasn't looking for a lesson in Plumbing 101, and she surely didn't know that he would need a degree in rocket science to understand what she wanted. The sink was leaking, it needed to be fixed, and, without question, he should have offered to fix it.

That's not what the guys at the conference thought, though.

"We're not mind readers," one exclaimed. "How was he supposed to know she wanted him to fix the sink?" another demanded. "Why didn't you just ask him to fix it?" one brother said, all flustered.

And we sistahs all looked at him like he was out of his natural born mind.

We figure that men are supposed to just get it—to know that the dishes need washing, to take the garbage out before it gets to smelling, not after it stinks up the place, and, yes, to know that if the sink in your lady friend's house is leaking, that you need to get out your tool belt, drop to your knees, and get that wrench a workin'.

And why should we expect anything less?

It's 2000, doggonit, and in this here new millennium, it only makes sense that men stop acting like we're still in the 1800s, when we women did all of the household chores and child-rearing, and the men simply reaped the benefits of a clean house and quiet, well-kept babies. I don't need to tell you that today, we women are working outside the household more than ever, in some cases making just as much money, if not more, than the men with whom we share our lives, which means that we're working more than ever because we've added that extra burden of earning a wage onto our child-rearing and household responsibilities.

What added responsibilities have you men gotten in the past 200 years? I say not a whole lot. Sure, the illusion is that more men are assuming the day-to-day familial responsibilities that come when wifey is off slaving like a workhorse on the modern-day plantations disguised as jobs. But the fact of the matter is that men seem only to perform what is deemed the traditional "female" roles when they *absolutely* have no other choice but to do it. That means that though you may wipe the kids' snotty noses and change their stinkin' diapers, you only do it when I'm either not around to do it, or I have to damn near beg and plead for you to do it. I mean, we could be kneeling in the middle of the living room floor, begging God to give us six extra sets of hands so that we can go get the milk, cheese, eggs, cereal, butter, and condoms, understand the kids' algebra lessons, fry the chicken without it burning, change the baby's diaper before the poopy goes clean up her back, and, "Please, Lord, let me get it done before, like, one A.M., so that I can finish up that memo for my boss before I get my two hours of sleep and start all over again tomorrow"—and the only thing you guys will offer to do is get right on down to the Rite Aid so that you can pick up—you guessed it—the condoms. "Don't want the store to close before we get those," you'll say, serious as a heart attack, a twinkle in the eye, like you've somehow figured out how I can schedule in 15 minutes sometime between 2 A.M. and 4 A.M. to give you some before I settle in for the night.

We definitely don't get that. We see the dishes need washing, we wash them. We know we're getting down to our last pair of clean jeans, we do the laundry. We know the kids need help with their homework, we sit down and help them sort it out. We know the family needs to eat dinner sometime before the evening ends, we cook.

Basically, we just do it.

You guys don't.

And we are constantly wondering why. I mean, at this point, we shouldn't have to *ask* you to help around the house; at this point, it should be apparent to you that there simply are things that *need* to be done and you should be one of the two people in the house doing them. No one should have to tell you or ask you or wish you into doing the obvious.

It doesn't, however, seem to be obvious to you all.

Why do we always have to ask you guys to do something, like buy the milk or change the baby's diaper or wash the dishes in the sink? Surely, you recognize that the chores and child-rearing need to be done and that it took two people to dirty up the house and make those babies.

From a Brother

Speaking on behalf of the brotherhood of man, I have one question: Were you all born perpetually unhappy and dissatisfied, or are you fitted with the pissed-off gene when you exchange the wedding vows and walk down the aisle?

Is my beautiful, squirming, little baby girl I'm currently holding in my arms already carrying around the genotype that will turn her into a nagging curmudgeon once she locates and secures the man of her dreams? The nagging wife is a stereotype that we have beaten into the ground in our society, but its genesis came from the idea that we have to search far and wide to find a woman who is happy with her man and his contribution to the household. Some women develop quite a bit more of the whine in their voices than others and put more menace in that snarl they conjure up whenever their man is around. These are the Nags with a capital N. But it seems that virtually every member of the gender has a little nag in them. Every one of you can find a reason to be pissed off at your man even as the lottery official is handing you that $10 million lottery check—"Honey, why didn't you clean out the car so that we'll have room to fit the $20,000 fur coat I've just decided to buy?" "Dear, that tie doesn't match those shoes, and you have a stain on your shirt."

In no single area is the dissatisfaction more pronounced and the nag more nurtured than with chores and household responsibilities. No matter how much we accomplish out in the world, no matter how many people look up to us in awe, the second we pass through the front doors of our home we transform, in your eyes, into Semi-Retarded Neanderthal Man, who has just mastered the art of walking upright and who responds to commands with barely more than an indecipherable grunt. And it doesn't really matter how much work we actually do in the house—to our women it's all relative and it's never enough. The man who sits around scratching his ass, watching every sporting contest ever invented, and letting go the beer burps during commercials is not inferior to the guy who strains to stay ahead of his wife's needs, giving himself headaches every night from watching her facial expressions to see if he's done enough housework yet or if she's about to find the one thing that he hasn't gotten around to doing. The wife of the first guy might look at the second guy and dream about him as the

Ideal Husband, but the moment she found herself sharing a marital bed with Ideal Husband, her frame of reference would change and she'd start finding all the things he isn't, all the stuff he forgot to do. Many guys discover this at an early age and figure it's not worth killing themselves over because the woman's never going to be happy anyway. Others of us keep at it, trying our damnedest to predict the source of her next complaint and take care of it preemptively—only to find ourselves failing time and again as the vitriol rains down on our heads.

What we quickly discover is that we lose all moral authority when we step through that front door. You can harangue us about the overflowing garbage can or the baby's dirty diapers, but we better not dare to attempt to turn the tables. Imagine how that would look: We slide the forkful of mashed potatoes into our mouth and turn up our nose in disgust. "Damn, honey, why'd you put so much salt in here?! Would you please learn how to cook the mashed potatoes like my mother does, okay?!" Like Eddie Murphy urged the kiddies when he was playing the lead character in the *Saturday Night Live* skit called "Mister Robinson's Neighborhood," I ask the men out there to go try this line on their women. Did she smack the mess out of you? You must have said it right.

A main reason why we never have the upper hand when it comes to household moral authority is because we're always playing catch-up/make-up. We're always in house detention, scrambling to make up that missed assignment or make amends for that spitball that hit its target. I didn't spend a whole lot of time in detention during my school years, but while I was there I don't recall finding it appropriate to raise my hand and ask the teacher why she never washes her car or still hasn't figured out how to activate the house alarm. In other words, after being on the receiving end of a critical mass of nagging, we've already screwed up too many times in your eyes to ever feel comfortable criticizing you for anything.

Our position sort of reminds me of the complaints you sometimes hear from white people who claim that black people are never satisfied—we're always pissed off about something. They think they've done something so sensitive and incredibly kind that the whole lot of black folk will stand up and wildly applaud them; instead what they hear is grousing that it's still not enough, "and where's our forty acres and a mule, anyway?!" That's how men feel. No, our women don't expect 40 acres and a mule, they're just waiting for the day when we can read their minds to anticipate each of their wishes before they even become wishes and willingly strip the dirty clothes off our children's backs before the sun has even set so we can rush to the washing machine and keep the kiddies looking clean and fresh.

There's a reason that the nag usually comes in the wife package rather than the girlfriend package: You keep the nag thoroughly suppressed until you get his chicken scratch of a signature on the marriage certificate. You know that the nag is what every boyfriend is searching desperately to find in the girlfriend before he dares produce an engagement ring. If we get nag from the girlfriend, once she becomes the wife she'll perfect the nag to such an art that she'd probably start sounding like Edith Bunker. We'd set fire to our testicles before we'd knowingly marry Edith Bunker. You are aware of this, so you manage somehow to excise the nag from your speech patterns during the girlfriend stage. You even pull off the neat trick of replacing the nag with a sex drive during this stage. In other words, you make yourself into the Ideal Woman. But when you attach that Mrs. to the front of your name, you step back into that phone booth and get restocked with a full tank of nag. Of course, the female body doesn't seem equipped to accommodate a full tank of nag and a robust sex drive—they cancel each other out like those plusses and minuses in algebra class. So what we are left with is that creature we all know so well: Wife.

If you ask us to do something and we do it, why isn't that good enough?

From a Sistah

Because you either take too long to do it, you don't do it the way we would like you to do it, or you do it half-assed so that we won't ask you to do it again. None of those ways will make us happy. You all seem to recognize this, but do it anyway so that your hands will never, ever have to touch the dishwater again, or the babies' diapers, or the dirty clothes basket, or anything else that remotely has to do with household chores and child-rearing. And then, like a whiny little boy who resorts to name-calling when he realizes he just got caught cheating, you all fall back on that nag thing.

Come on, admit it: Y'all know how y'all do. My brother Troy was an expert at it—schooled me really early on the ways of a man who doesn't want to do jack around the house. I can remember clearly several times when, as youngsters, my mother would order me to do the chores that Troy had previously been ordered to do because bro didn't get the job done right. If my mother told him to wash the dishes, he'd leave some eggs caked up at the bottom of the frying pan or break a glass or two, knowing full well that my mother would look upon his efforts with clear disdain and disgust. Mommy hated nasty dishes, and she especially didn't really trust too many kids around her good china, and Troy knew this—so his leaving the dishes a little dirty and his dropping a few glasses here and there virtually assured that he'd never again get his turn at the sink.

Soon, it was my job exclusively.

Same went for the laundry. My brother would find a way to get some bleach into the dark clothes, or go out of his way to make sure the iron was just a little too hot for one of Mommy's silk shirts, and the next thing you knew, no more washing and ironing for Troy.

Soon, that, too, was my job exclusively.

Ditto for the mopping of the floors, the general dusting of the furniture, the cleaning of the bathrooms, the vacuuming of the steps, the cutting of the lawn. And as he got each one of his assignments deducted from his list of chores, he got extra time added to his playtime with the boys. Me? I was Cinder-freakin'-rella, because it pained me to *not* do it right. Troy knew what he was doing.

You guys do, too.

Like, if your woman asks you to do something simple, like comb your boy's hair and get your little girl dressed for school, we can't help but think that you deliberately left his head looking like a bowl of peas and put her in a purple-checked top with a red polka-dot skirt because you know that the crazier the kids look, the less chance I'll ask you to get them dressed tomorrow—or, even better, I won't ever depend on you to get them dressed again. Why else would you dress the girl like that? *You* certainly know better than to walk out the house looking like a Salvation Army special (or at least some of you do), so there *has* to be only one reason why you would let your kid be seen like that in public. So you won't ever be asked to do it again.

That's not to say that some of you don't mean well. There are certainly those of you who really do try hard to get what we asked you to do done. Problem is, you just don't do it like we'd like you to do it. I know, I know—this is purely our problem, not yours, but it's real and it's bothersome and it's hard to deal with, from both our perspectives. Take, for instance, the way that Nick handles Mari's crying fits. I mean, to me, it's not all that difficult; she's upset, she wants comforting, I comfort her in the way she likes to be comforted. Head in the crook of my arm, body across my chest, my hand gently patting her bottom, slow, steady bounce, soothing whispers— "It's okay baby, don't cry." It's a science passed on to me by my mother, who taught me the walk, my mother-in-law, who taught me the talk, and my sister-in-law, who taught me the pat and bounce. It took me some time to get it, but now? I'm the master.

Nick? He holds her in the air with one hand, or holds her with both hands at arm's-length like she's a stinky diaper, or, the one I hate the most, just sits her on his lap and lets her cry until she passes out from exhaustion and sleeps it off. It works for him (kinda). It does not work for me (ever). As far as I'm concerned, if the baby is still crying, she's not being comforted, and if she's not being comforted, then she's uncomfortable, and if she's uncomfortable, then I feel bad, and if I feel bad, I need to take her back so that I can make both her and me feel better. I recognize that this is unfair, because he has his own way of doing things, or so my friends and all the parenting books tell me. "He's not doing it wrong; he's doing it his way," my girlfriend Cathy told me. "Just leave the room and let Daddy do his thing."

We just can't. Been the chief care-givers from the giddy-up and giving up the way we do it 90 percent of the time to let him feel comfortable doing it his way during his 10 percent of the care-giving time just doesn't—and never will—fly.

You need to accept this.

Nothing, however, irks us more than when we ask you guys to do something, and you guys take your sweet time doing it. This is, perhaps, most annoying of all, because we can accept the fact that you might just be getting-the-kids-dressed–challenged, or simply unable to comfort the baby. But there's just no excuse for performing a task that we know you can do hours after we ask you to do it. One of my office girlfriends told me the story of her pregnancy, which pretty much involved being crouched over the toilet 23 hours a day, six days a week. On the 24th hour and the seventh day, you could usually find her either sleeping or sipping on ginger ale and sucking down crackers to keep the upchuck down. So there were a lot of things that were going undone around the house, mostly because she just didn't have the energy to do them. At the top of that list was the dishes, which seemed to never get washed—no matter if they'd been left in the sink for days at a time—unless she dragged herself into the kitchen and did them between prayers to the porcelain God. At one point, she told me that she deliberately didn't wash the dishes, just to see how long her man would go without washing them before she had to ask him to do it. After five days, there weren't even any more clean glasses in the house, and still, he didn't once think to wash the dishes. When she finally asked him to do it, he angrily mumbled that he was going to do it when he got a chance, then proceeded to leave them in the sink another day before he broke down and did them.

"What the hell is that all about?" girlfriend asked.

Listening to our conversation was a co-worker of mine, a man's man if you will, the kind of guy who sits at home in his underwear on Sundays, a beer in one hand, the remote in the other, scratching and burping and carrying on while he peruses the *TV Guide* for the Sunday NFL lineup.

Man's Man's jumbled explanation was something about how men don't want to be told what to do, particularly when they're in the middle of doing something. His wife, he said, had a special knack for asking him to do stuff while he was watching the game, then getting mad because he didn't immediately get up and do it. "Makes me move even slower," he said before walking back to his desk. I could have sworn his knuckles were dragging on the floor as he moved.

The one thing you need to understand here is that if we ask you to do something, we've pretty much been thinking about it, pondering it, and turning it around in our minds for quite a while—knowing full well that you have no intentions on doing it because you've walked past it so many times without doing it that tracks have worn into the carpet. And before we break down and ask you to do it, we wonder which tack you'll take—whether you'll do it wrong on purpose, or do it in a way different from the way we would have done it—and then we'll get disgusted and wonder if we should do it ourselves. Then we'll resign ourselves to the fact that we just don't have time to do it, because if we did, it would have been done already, and then we go on ahead and take our chances by asking you to just do it.

And then we sit back and wait for you to move your ass and get to doing what we asked you to do *right now* or else—the "or else" being us getting disgusted by your not moving fast enough and just doing it our damn selves.

Inevitably, you guys don't move fast enough, and we quickly get into the "or else" mode. And if we bother to complain?

Nags.

Just how fair is that? Not very, I'd argue. A lot of us women are constantly on the lookout for this—sidestepping, backsliding, ducking in every which way to avoid being labeled as whiny, screeching, can't-ever-be-pleased wives who do everything within their power to make their men miserable. So we ask nicely, sweetly, syrupy. We bribe. We cajole. We come forth with heads bowed, trying our best to make the request in such a way that will not offend or bother you. Basically, we throw away everything our proud mamas, Oprah, and Iyanla ever told us about being strong black women, and we yield to you the power to make us feel bad for asking you to perform such mundane womanly tasks, like watching the baby or changing her diaper or fixing supper for a change. One of my new-mother girlfriends and I got to talking one day about how ridiculous we feel asking our husbands to watch the kids while we do what most every human being does during the course of the day, and how their reactions just piss us off to the highest of pistivity. Like the time she wanted to take a dump, and she found herself saying to her husband, "Could you just watch him for just a couple minutes—I have to go to the bathroom."

"The way I said it was just so mealy-mouthed," she said, quite disgusted with herself. "I mean, everybody has to take a shit, right? I felt bad asking him to watch the baby so that I could have five minutes in the bathroom to relieve myself, even though I'd been watching the baby *all day long*. And he had the nerve to act like I'd just told him I was going out with the girls and I'd be back in a couple of days."

She went on to say that she avoids asking him to do anything with the baby, or to give up some of his worktime to be with his new family, because the last thing she wants her husband to think is that she's a nag. No matter that she doesn't see him for days on end or that she is raising her child damn near like a single mother. To keep her husband from thinking she's a nag, she's just willing to deal.

And that's messed up.

Sometimes though, we just don't give a hoot about the "N" word—and I certainly can relate. Mari was attached to my tit and my hip for, oh, a good three days straight, and though I love the girl with all my heart and I would kill with my bare hands the person who dared to muss one single strand of hair on her head, I needed to get away from her. Just for a few minutes. The dishes in the sink were piled up—had been for that same three days—and the newspapers were spread all across the living room and sitting areas and the baby's room, and I just needed to put her down, straighten up, and exhale. But Nick was in the room, writing, which he does the majority of his days while I find things to do with the baby until I get in my three hours of writing time. I didn't want to ask him to take her, but I had to—for her sake, my sake, everybody's sanity. I figured I'd wash the dishes to ease my tension. Wash the dishes, y'all. Like, the highlight of my damn day is to bend over a sinkful of dishes.

And when I asked my sweet, adoring, usually-above-and-be-yond-helpful husband if he could watch Mari "just for a minute," boyfriend rolled his eyes, eyed the clock, threw out a sigh, and said, "What for?"

What for? What the hell for? What did it matter? I was asking him to watch our child. I didn't care if I was about to take a trip to Timbuktu to watch the international Watusi dance troupe perform the Harlem jig—I didn't feel like I had to justify why I was asking my baby daddy to watch his child. Just take her, dammit.

And then I got attitudinal.

And I'm sure that he said to himself, "Self? My wife is a complete and total nag with a capital 'N'."

But you know what? I didn't give a damn. If my asking my husband to help with the baby for a few minutes while I take the time to check myself classified me as a nag, then so be it. I'm a nag. But on those few occasions when I am, my dishes are clean, my child's behind has been wiped, and I have gotten what I wanted to get done done.

Why is it that when a woman asks you to do something that you don't necessarily want to do, you all accuse her of causing trouble—of being the nag?

From a Brother

Well, damn. Now I see what my woman really thinks about me. Not only do I hold my child like she is a dirty diaper, but I have the nerve to ask her why she needs me to take the baby during the time slot we agreed would be mine to get writing done. This is all yet another monumental example of each side failing to see things from the other's perspective.

I think what bothers us most about jumping like an army private to our wives' requests is that it's all her agenda, pulled from her schedule, to be done in her time frame. In effect, we have lost control of our own time, and we are dangling like a marionette with our wives handling the strings. This is a very disconcerting feeling, one that we will struggle against until the end of time. I think it's a quite human and adult response to be somewhat annoyed when another person interrupts our peaceful repose to tell us to do something that is not what we have chosen to be doing at the time. It's especially annoying when it's part of some waiting game that the spouse is playing to see how adept we will be at reading her mind. Though my wife keeps repeating our failures at detecting dirty dishes or clothes, it's still a question of whose agenda we choose to respond to. Our agenda might entail taking out the garbage when it's full rather than when it contains something that our wife thinks is smelly; we might very well decide to wash the dishes when we run out of clean glasses rather than when there are just two dirty plates resting at the bottom of the sink. Much of this is a function of our backgrounds, our childhoods, what we are used to. If our mothers didn't make us wash the dishes until the dirty ones covered every inch of kitchen counter space, then that's the standard we're going to bring into a relationship—even if it drives our wife crazy. For instance, my wife and I have different standards about how many dirty clothes can be left lying around the room before it becomes an eyesore—I have always been particular about folding or hanging up my clothes or placing them in the dirty clothes hamper. Denene, on the other hand, doesn't seem to know what a dirty clothes hamper is, or she mistakenly believes our entire bedroom is a dirty clothes hamper. But I'm not going to spend many precious waking hours preoccupied with the location of Denene's clothes and why she hasn't picked them up in the past week. That's where the nag label comes from—in two equivalent situations, you voice your displeasure over and over again while we just accept your shortcomings and keep strolling.

And I think it's unfair to judge the behavior of adult men by what strategies a little boy who happened to be your brother used 20 years ago to get out of chores. How ridiculous is it to suppose that a man would send his daughter out in public looking like a mismatched clown because he didn't want to be saddled anymore with the task of getting her dressed in the morning? Talk about passive-aggressive psychopathology—that would be worthy of a trophy from the American Psychiatric Association. We might be motivated by a desire to finish as soon as possible, but the last thing most of us want after completing the task is for you to come scurrying behind us muttering under your breath about our incompetence and how you can't count on us to do anything right. Being trapped in one of those situations raises the hair on the backs of our necks. As opposed to your brother, I was committed during my childhood years to doing my best at any task I was asked to do, to the point where my mother often asked me to wash the dishes rather than my older sister, who would scowl and sulk her way all the way through it. I'm sure your brother did all sorts of crazy things as a little boy that he wouldn't do now. So did I and a million other guys.

There's a danger in the let's-see-how-long-it-takes-him-to-get-around-to-it approach to household chores. For one, it assumes that we are orbiting in the same solar system as you, that we are attuned to the same household needs and want to tend to them in the same time frame. As I have said before, if we are spending our waking hours worried sick about the state of the boiler in the dead of winter, we might be less inclined to notice the dishes piling up in the sink. But in the back of our head we know how upset you'd be if you woke up the next morning with a layer of frost coating your ass. You'd blame that on us and wonder why we didn't pay closer attention to the boiler. And we'd be foolish if we just stood around as the boiler struggled on its last leg and waited for you to come down in the basement and get down on your knees to keep an eye on the pilot light. That's just not likely to happen. But let us go a day or two without tackling the dishes and we become the most boorish husband ever to walk the earth.

Can't we just agree to meet in the middle? You need me to do something, you ask me to do it when I'm able. I need you to do something, I do the same for you. Sounds simple to me.

9

In Corporate America: Does It Matter Who's on Top?

From a Sistah

I wanted to just come off the stage and smack him. Hard.

Because this brother was arguing, in effect, that racism does not affect black women, that we should be as happy as pigs in—well, you know—and that sistahs everywhere from the welfare line to the corporate boardroom should simply get over any anxiety we have about blackness and white men because we don't suffer like African-American men do. "In fact," he said, quite smugly, "white men use you to get at us.

"You have no idea what it's like to be a black man in America," he continued. "We are constantly emasculated by white men, and ninety-nine percent of the time, it will be a black woman he uses to do it."

Alrighty, then.

Nick looked at him, then at me, then handed over the mike—and just sort of settled in his chair. He knew this was going to be a heated exchange. Any black man who dared to tell this black woman that she was untouched by racism in America and that her studying and degrees and constant do-right mentality made her a pawn in the emasculation of African-American men was going to get told off on this particular day.

And why wouldn't I—or any self-respecting sistah, for that matter—argue him down? We get sick and tired of that same ol' "oh woe is the black man in America" speech, the one in which the self-righteous, red-black-and-green-flag-carrying, in-between-jobs, ain't-never-read-a-book-but-heard-about-it-on-*Like It Is* scholar brother proudly and loudly steps on the necks of black women to justify why his life sucks.

I know not all you brothers are like that, but there are way too many of you who do think that your suffering is somehow more painful than that of black women in America. So let me provide you this news flash—you know, set things straight.

Cabs pass us by, too.

We get followed around the store, too.

Police give us nasty glares and beat our behinds, too.

We get dogged out by the media, too (can match every one of your evening news black-male-perp-walk shots with an image of a fat, greasy black woman as welfare queen or toothless, pink-curler-clad- "I seent it" eyewitness).

We get passed up for promotions, too—by the same white boy that we trained six months ago.

And we, too, wonder why white folks can't just get over it and move on already.

All this is to say that if a black woman has a position of power in the workplace, rest assured that it was no easy feat for her to get there, just as it was no easy feat for any black man to get his corporate nod.

Still, that doesn't stop brothers from assuming that all the corporate jobs open to minorities are given only to black women so that the boss can A) satisfy two categories on his equal employment opportunity survey (black, woman) and B) get back at all the black men of America.

Uh-huh.

I would argue that while there may be a few instances in which white, male corporate officials have promoted black women to satisfy a double quota, most of the sistahs holding those positions of power got them for working hard, and deserve them. They studied, they got their degrees, they struggled to climb the corporate ladder, and they snatched that golden ring as best they could *despite* the obstacles thrown in their way, just like many of the brothers in those same powerful positions.

And the white men who put them there? Oh, they're not comfortable with the black corporate sistahs, either. Sure, they may be more comfortable with the sistah than the brother, as the brother could be a serious test of manhood to a man who doesn't feel he quite measures up. (Don't all guys feel this way about other guys anyway, no matter what color they are?) But I guarantee you that that white man isn't completely comfortable, either, with the black woman. To him, she is what society makes her out to be: She is angry, mean, and sassy, but not all that smart. When he walks into a meeting with her, she is listened to, but barely—because you can't really take what she has to say too seriously. But don't tell her that, for God's sake, because she'd cuss you out. And there will be nothing you can do about it, because you can't fire a double minority. Let's leave her there for show.

This does not make sistahs happy. To be in a position of power, but treated like a low-class intern, just isn't what most of us spent all that time learning and training and studying and praying for. We simply want to do the job, and have someone tell us, "Job well done."

Still, we get pointed out by our own as traitors to the race—colluding in the white man's evil agenda to rid the earth of the black male species. The evil plan? Make all the black men have to answer to African-American female bosses.

How utterly ridiculous.

Why, may I ask, do black men always assume that the only reason black women are in executive positions is because some white man decided to use her to get back at a black man?

From a Brother

This whole debate has gotten so tiresome to me, but yet it will continue to rage on for as long as there are brothers out there who need to explain to the world why they are standing on the corner at two in the afternoon instead of collecting a paycheck. People who are in dire straits have a very desperate, human need to find scapegoats—a reason for their failures. For black men, one of the handiest targets is that sistah striding through the office like she's God's gift to the corporate world and who would look suspiciously down her nose at any brother she happened to find sitting across her desk on a job interview. When that job is denied us, we will tell everyone who will listen for the next decade that it's because of the sistahs that we haven't been able to buy that Mercedes.

It is unsettling and counterproductive to get into that tortured debate about who is more aggrieved and despised in American society, the black man or the black woman, but there are a few things that sistahs should be able to agree with us on. First of all, you don't need a Ph.D. in African-American history to understand that white society has historically been more comfortable working in close proximity to black women than to black men. For heaven's sake, they entrust black women with the monumental task of raising their children—a relationship doesn't get more comfortable and trusting than that. (When I developed a close friendship during my years at Yale with a white boy who grew up amidst wealth on New York City's Upper East Side, I told him the reason we got along so well was because we were both raised by black women.) It isn't much of a leap in logic to extend that comfort into the workplace. We don't even need to delve much into white society's historical relationship with the black man except to say that it wasn't quite as comfortable and trusting. Fear and trembling much more accurately describe the mutual feelings between white society and black men.

I don't want anyone to suggest that I am in any way trying to downplay the hard work and successes of black women in the corporate world. Of course the sistahs have to work ten times harder and be ten times better than their white counterparts to make any kind of significant advancement. They're not *that* comfortable with you in the workplace. They're going to look at every other candidate three or four extra times before they turn to you for the big promotion—unless of course they have a lawsuit pending or the judgmental eyes of some watchdog group peering in at them. I think when most black men drag up this issue, what they are seeking from the sistahs is an acknowledgment of these facts—an acknowledgment that rarely comes. According to statistics compiled by the U.S. Census Bureau, not only were there nearly a million more black women than black men in the workforce in 1998 (the latest year for which figures were available), but there were over 600,000 more black women than black men in positions that the census described as executive, administrative, managerial, or professional. These are the kinds of supervisory jobs in corporate America to which most of us are aspiring. There were 1.78 million black women in these positions in 1998, while there were 1.16 million black men.

Most brothers have encountered the harsh condemning glare of a successful corporate sistah who is quick to judge us by the clothes on our back or the earring in our ear and conclude that we are beneath her and not even worthy of another glance. We can see the disgust in her eyes, the tense brace of her body, and we know she has decided that not only is she better than us but heaven help us if we ever walked into her office looking for a job.

After my sophomore year in college, I felt lucky to snag a job as a messenger for a high-priced Wall Street law firm. It was one of those exquisitely decorated law factories, with several hundred associates toiling away in offices that seemed to stretch for miles down tasteful marble corridors. The summer associates programs in these places are out of this world, with students from the nation's top law schools eagerly flocking to the firm to have their nights filled with fancy dinners with senior partners and weekends packed with raucous parties at one partner or another's Hamptons beach house. There were very few black summer associates there during my time at the firm, but there was a very beautiful sistah who was studying at Berkeley's law school, Boalt Hall. From the first day, this lovely sistah went as far out of her way as she could to ignore me. If we passed each other in the corridors she quickly would look the other way. Once when we were alone in the elevator together, I summoned up the courage to say "Hello" to her. She looked stunned and troubled, shocked that I would dare try to engage her in conversation and concerned that someone else might see the exchange. She mumbled something inaudible in response and practically sprinted off the elevator when it reached her floor—I *think* it was her floor. After a few weeks, I resigned myself to the fact that sistahs like her were off-limits to even my gestures of common courtesy.

But toward the end of the summer, only a few days before I was to leave and return to Yale, this sistah stepped onto the elevator, saw me standing there, *and gave me a big toothy smile*. I almost wanted to look around and make sure there wasn't someone else aboard that she was smiling at. I gave her an uncomfortable little smile in return. Then she said, "So, I hear you're a junior at Yale. What are you majoring in?" She was all bubbly and warm, even sounding more like a black girl than I'd ever heard her during the previous three months. I understood right away what had happened and I was disgusted. Someone had given her some information about me and she realized I wasn't some black boy who'd be spending the rest of his life in the messenger room—I was already somewhat accomplished and thus worthy of her conversation and maybe even friendship. I learned a painful but important lesson that day about the way that black men are viewed by the rest of the world, including our own sistahs.

We care deeply what other people think about us, even if we try so hard to pretend we don't. I think the trouble starts when brothers feel like the black women who surround them settle into some newly attained position in corporate America and then look around and wonder why the brothers aren't doing as well for themselves. It starts feeling like the questions that Asian or European or Caribbean immigrants ask about us, only months after arriving here and securing a bank loan for their own business or their own house. "I did it—why can't you?" they wonder. We see the sistahs making the same query of us and our instinctive reaction is to remind them of the history, the baggage, the prejudice that has been our nemesis for centuries. None of this is to say that black women haven't suffered too and don't continue to suffer. The point is that the history of black women in America and thus their current position in corporate America is a different one from ours, not to be put side by side and gauged for whose suffering is worse. We have both suffered, but our stories are not the same.

We continue to argue about who is more favored by the white man—black men or black women. Why do women have such a hard time with the suggestion that employers would much rather hire a black woman and get two minorities in one?

From a Sistah

We can accept that in some instances, this does happen. But certainly not every woman holding a corporate position was put there to fulfill a double-minority quota.

I have to admit that I was quite shocked the first time one of my white male superiors suggested as much. One of my black male colleagues, bored with himself and his job, was contemplating either becoming a columnist at our newspaper or quitting and writing books full-time. They are the dreams of most writers—to be able to say whatever the hell you want to say in a major U.S. newspaper, or be able to sustain a living saying whatever the hell you want to say in books—and my colleague, in the business for well over a decade and a half, decided it was time to make that move. He is a beautiful, gifted writer, a true mentor to me, and I figured I'd help him out a little by going into the boss's office and arguing on his behalf. I mean, to me, it made perfect sense; at our newspaper, every columnist was—and at this sitting, still is—a white,

Irish male. I was sure that our readers—myself included—would have found it quite refreshing to hear the opinions of someone else for a change, whether it was an African American, Asian, Native American, or Martian. So this I argued to the boss man. And just as I shocked him by suggesting my colleague (Mr. Boss thought I'd cornered him to do my own bidding) become the new columnist, so did Mr. Boss shock me by saying he'd like to give me the job.

My jaw dropped; I could barely contain my excitement. I wanted to call Nick and my daddy, and tell them the good news.

Then, Mr. Boss dropped my high like a drug dealer does to a crackhead who asks for a hit on credit. First, the insult: "If you're the new columnist, then I'd have a black and a woman. Can't beat that," he said, a wry grin crossing his lips. Then came the letdown: "I don't want to talk about this with you just yet because you're pregnant and you'll be on maternity leave sooner than you know it, and who knows when you'll be back? Can't start something you won't be able to finish."

Just like that—a one-two beat down with both the insult stick and the stupid stick. Mr. Boss had, in effect, denied the job to my colleague, an African-American male, by dangling it before me, an African-American female. And then, right behind it, he snatched the job away from me, too.

See what I'm saying here? We were both victims—my mentor for not being a double minority, and me for being one. Neither of us got the job, and neither of us probably ever will. So who is hurting more here, him or me? I'd argue that we both lose, as does the newspaper, because in just a couple of minutes of contemplation, a person who had the power to add a voice to New York City's most read newspaper shot it down. And I could easily say that I lost out because I am a woman, since no man will ever have a pregnancy or kids handed to him as an excuse for why he can't move up the corporate ladder.

There is, however, something more troubling about the question here: There is an assumption that a black woman in power is somehow a hindrance to black men. I would argue that a woman with a higher authority at a job would be a blessing to black men, as she would be the one to give your black behind some juice in the company. I mean, couldn't black men look to her as a mentor, a person they could turn to when job problems arise, or they, too, want to move on up in the company, or simply to provide an ear and a shoulder to lean on when things get stupid? Sure, one could easily argue that it's those corporate negroes you gotta watch out for—they'll be the first ones to sell your soul to the devil, then sit down to the table and help him eat you alive—but in my time, I've come across way more black men and women in positions of power willing to help me get my career on than those who would bite off their own tongues rather than help a brother or a sistah out. Shoot, it was a network of brothers who helped me get to where I am today, and I thank God they got their positions every day of my life because if they hadn't suffered, sacrificed, and climbed before me, I wouldn't be writing these words. I'm sure that there are some black men out there who feel the same way about a sistah who made the same sacrifices, then turned around and lent them a hand up.

Let's not avoid some sobering statistics, since we done got me started: According to the U.S. Census Bureau, black men still make a much higher income than black women at all levels of educational attainment. For college graduates, black men earned a median annual salary of $35,290 in 1998, while black women earned $30,864. (White men were the highest at $49,018, while white women barely edged out black women at $30,927.) Basically, black women are still at the bottom of the totem pole in corporate America, and it hardly seems that anyone—not even most black men—are offering to help *us* up, despite what a lot of brothers think.

Now, you would figure that you all would be first on line, trying to help us be all we can be. But all too often, we sistahs are asked—no, ordered—to step aside and let black men receive their glory. That order usually comes couched in the lopsided argument that it is more important for black women to fight for the rights of African Americans than it is for them to fight for the rights of women. And what happens when we do that? Sistahs end up catching the wrath from both racists and sexists, except to me, the sexism is more hurtful than the racism because at least I can expect the racism. The sexism from the very men that I was brought up to love and respect—black men—is more hurtful than any kind of nigger craziness some white boy could ever put me through.

Which is more of a threat to black men—a white man in power, or a black woman in power?

From a Brother

The white man in power is the devil we know; the black woman in power is one gigantic question mark. She may become another devil we know, or she may be a great boon to our lives and careers. But we have reason to approach her with suspicion. I must say from experience that I never know what to expect when I encounter a sistah in a position of power. You ask whether we have met sistahs willing to lend a helping hand to a brother in need, and the answer is yes, most of us have. But we have also encountered many sistahs playing the role of the Official Negro Bouncer, who sees it as her job to keep all the unsavory-looking black folk from passing through the company's front doors—and if she messes up and lets a few inside, she watches them like a hawk so she'll be prepared to toss them out on their asses at the first scent of trouble. Don't let any supplies turn up missing or the vending machine appear to be tampered with—the Bouncer will sprint to that black man she wasn't so sure about and question him so vociferously that homeboy would rather be interrogated by Brooklyn cops. Just as with the black cop, the whites in the Bouncer's company won't give her tactics a second thought. After all, that's what she was appointed to do, weed out the unsavory negroes.

It goes without saying that these "unsavory negroes" usually happen to be black males, with whom her comfort level just isn't as high as with the females.

And heaven forbid if brotherman hasn't been schooled yet about the idiosyncracies of the workplace when he steps into her office for an interview. He may have a sterling transcript and appear to be an eager worker, but he never had anyone around to show him how to properly knot a tie or shine his shoes. Every warning light in the Bouncer's body starts flashing and her "ghetto sensor" starts whooping like a banshee. Needless to say, the job will not be his. A white male recruiter might have looked at his transcript and observed his eagerness and decided to give the boy a chance. The black woman cuts him off on the suspicion that the boy will join the company and proceed to embarrass her with his cheap suits and awkward manners. To make it worse, the less experienced brothers among us may make the mistake of letting down their guard when they see the sistah behind the desk, assuming their task has just become easier. Little do they know.

I've had black female supervisors in the past, as well as white male and white female supervisors. It would be dangerous to generalize based on my one sample, but things were certainly a lot more complicated with the black females. In addition to all the baggage she carried by being a female boss supervising male employees, she also had to find a way to deal with race so that the whites she also supervised wouldn't accuse her of giving preferential treatment to the black boy—and the black boy didn't think she was unnecessarily hard on him. In the case of my black female supervisors, they usually erred in the direction of being harder on me than my peers. It was so annoying to me that I must admit there were times when I longed for the simplicity of an uncaring white boy giving me the orders.

What all this means is that we need to have more black women in positions of power so that they become more adept at it and less likely to bring cargo-loads of baggage into the job with them. And the more sistahs there are in these positions, the less likely they will be to feel that the whole world is looking over their shoulder, questioning their every move. But until we get there, I'm sure many a brother will find his heart beating a bit faster—and jumping up into his throat—when he steps into that interview room to find a sistah looking up at him with her eyebrows already raised.

Work Time vs. Face Time: Which Is More Important?

From a Sistah

You know what? We don't ask for much.

Just a little quality time.

And some help with the kids.

A little romance here and there.

Agreement to go to dinner at my mama's without giving us any lip.

And that you put the seat down.

But this appears to be beyond some brothers' reach. Because it requires some serious commitment. And attention. And occasional sacrifice.

Guys aren't very good at sacrifice.

Particularly when it gets in the way of their making money. Or getting a better position at their job. Or making money. Or achieving some sort of fame. Or one-upping the other guy. Or making more money.

Wife be damned. Kids be damned. Personal life be damned.

Got to make that money, get that promotion, make that money, get recognition for making that money, be better/smarter/faster/ stronger than that other guy, and make more money.

And this immediately presents itself as a problem for us. Because, like that chick Alex in *Fatal Attraction*, we don't like to be ignored. Can't stand to play second fiddle. Can't wrap ourselves around being alone. Particularly when we have a man. It's just not right.

You all know this. Yet you still do it. By going to work at 6 A.M., before the babies and the wife are awake. And coming home well after the macaroni and cheese has congealed, the roast chicken has dried out, the iced tea has gotten watery, and the babies have gone to bed, again without getting a good-night kiss from the man whose name—Daddy—is on their lips when their little heads head for the pillow and sleepyland. And spending the weekend helping her do laundry and, in the meantime, disappearing to do more work, only to resurface in time for bed, where you promptly try to get some.

This is played. Big time. Because what we're beginning to feel is the mother/maid/whore/bitch syndrome—the one in which we suffer hardy as we keep house, raise the kids, spread our legs when he's ready, and get pissed off because even though we are married, we feel alone. And used. And irrelevant.

We don't like this.

We can't like this.

But when we tell you this, you do nothing. You don't listen. You don't come home at night. You don't change your ways. Or remotely try. You give us the line. You know the one. The "I'm doing this for us, baby, so that we can have a better life" line. The "You knew this is how it was going to be" line. The "What did you expect" line.

And you swear up and down that you simply want us to be happy. "Why can't you just be happy, baby? All this is for you."

Well, we can't be happy.

Because the money is nothing without you.

The things are nothing without you.

The kids are nothing without you.

I am nothing without you.

I want you.

Here.

With me.

And the babies.

In our home.

Fuck the boss.

Why do so many men sacrifice time with the family to slave away at work?

From a Brother

When Time *magazine devoted a major portion of a 1999 issue to the crazy wealth flowing to all the young Internet entrepreneurs in Silicon Valley, one of the most mind-boggling sections for me focused on how the young men out there are so obsessed with making huge mounds of money that they don't have time for mundane matters like romance and women.*

"For most people, relationships are simply not time-effective," said one Silicon Valley executive. "People think having relationships with the opposite sex is nice, but if it gets in the way of making $3 million, forget it. They'll go to bars for a quick hit."

Sabeer Bhatia, the 31-year-old co-founder of Hotmail, who made $200 million when he sold his company to Microsoft in 1998, said he works 18 hours a day because it's fun.

"I've chosen a certain life, and I've been pretty successful," Bhatia said. *"For right now, success and marriage don't really mix."* These guys are just the most recent extreme of that time-honored male tradition of working so hard that everything else suffers. In Silicon Valley, they certainly aren't helped any by a single male–single female ratio of nearly 5,500 to one—though single women probably flocked to the Valley in droves after Time magazine told the nation how many single workaholic millionaires were spending their nights out there with only their hard drives to keep them company. This male money-making obsession, which we also discuss in other chapters, is so deeply rooted in our psyches that a roving flock of Jennifer Lopez look-alikes would have a hard time pulling us away from the office—so imagine the difficulty faced by our wives. (Just kidding.)

So many marriages have been reduced to a pile of rubble by this moneymaking obsession that you could build a looming skyscraper from their ashes. These doomed marriages can usually be spotted from a mile away—the husband-to-be can't even make it to the wedding rehearsal dinner on time because he had to work late to finish up a proposal, brief, memo, article, prospectus, project. . . . Homeboy even had to cut his bachelor party short because he had so much work to finish up before the honeymoon, which he spends on his cell phone the majority of the time while his new wife broils next to him on the beach. Once they get back home, she soon realizes that the honeymoon was the height of their time together because she has to schedule appointments to get any face time with her new husband. He comes to sleep and occasionally to screw, which soon leads to a new child arriving on the scene. That keeps her busy and sated for a while, until she realizes she's raising her kid on her own. She doesn't like this. She starts pestering him so much about his lack of quality time in the home that he starts avoiding her just so he doesn't have to hear her mouth. He buys her off with increasingly expensive presents that he is able to afford with his escalating compensation package. He's going to make partner, he thinks, if it kills him. And before it gets around to killing him, first it destroys his marriage. By the first kid's fourth birthday and the next kid's second, they are spending one night a week in marriage counseling—when he actually makes it there before the session time is up. To make matters worse, he has discovered golf, which happens to be the favorite pastime of his boss. Any daylight time not at the office is spent at the golf course. She doesn't like this, even if she does almost believe his claims that the golf will help his career. It takes another year before she starts asking around for the names of a few good divorce lawyers. The nasty legal battle takes another year to complete. Mr. Hardworking Family Man now has a new name: Zoo Dad—the moniker to match the usual destination during his children's bimonthly visits.

And it seems that the more successful Zoo Dad becomes, the more screwed up his kids will be. They act out to get his attention; he reacts to their acting out by becoming increasingly disgusted with the knuckleheads he sired and spending less and less time with them. It's all a vicious cycle doomed to be repeated over and over again. A few years ago, I went to a memorial service to commemorate the life of the influential man who ran *The Star-Ledger*, the last newspaper where I worked, a man whose hand reached into every corner of New Jersey to make or break politicians and champion or sink all sorts of statewide projects. I heard his son say something that nearly took my breath away. The son told the hundred or so people gathered at a grand hall in northern New Jersey that he didn't get to spend much time with his father when he was growing up. Here was a grown man speaking at a ceremony where the clear mandate was to say as many nice things as you can about the deceased, and his son took the occasion to grouse about the time they spent together. To me his statement pointed to a well-spring of bitterness that was probably bubbling just beneath the surface. I wondered how disturbed the father would have been to hear the son choose that fact as one of the most noteworthy things he could say about Dad. I wonder if any other men who heard that statement pledged to themselves on that day that they would never be so obsessed with work that their son could make a similar statement about them.

I understand the male desire to accumulate as much as he can to validate for himself and the watching world that his was a life of value and importance. This male drive can lead to many astounding accomplishments and staggering riches, but it can also create bitter disappointment and missed childhoods. It is up to every individual male to ask himself how much is enough and what he's willing to risk to get it. Every male has to decide what will be sacrificed and what must be saved and cherished. I understand that.

What I don't understand is how a woman can witness the single-minded obsession of an ambitious male, decide to hitch a ride to his shooting star, then complain once she gets him down the aisle that he's spending too much time on his ambition and not enough on her. If you meet the incredibly busy neurosurgeon at a friend's party, have a love connection, exchange the digits, and then have to take another month tracking him down as he spends virtually every waking hour with his fingers immersed in someone's gray matter, this should be an indication of what it will be like as his wife. If you hook up with the NBA star during his team's West

Coast swing, then you have to have a phone relationship with him for the next three months until he plays the Clippers again, don't you think he'll still have to do a little traveling after he marries you? In other words, when women meet the so-called man of their dreams, they usually know what they are getting before the exchange of vows. They know what he does for a living, they know how ambitious he is, they know how hard he works.

So why do women get the ring and then start to trip that he's not home enough?

From a Sistah

Because you all inevitably change the minute the ring is on our finger and the first sip of champagne hits the back of our throats—something we didn't bargain for when we agreed to do the "I do."

The fact of the matter is that when he's dating the woman he thinks he might want to spend the rest of his life with, he goes out of his way to make her happy. It's what we all do when we're trying to impress someone, isn't it? Do whatever we can to make them happy?

So this Wall Streeter gets enamored by this hottie he met at a mutual friend's dinner party. It's clear she's neither a hootchie nor an airhead Annie in search of a Daddy Warbucks. This girl's got it together—has her own good job, is reasonably intelligent, can hold a conversation, is brimming with class. He decides to get to know her better.

And he does.

With dinner. And dancing. And gifts. And long-lasting late night phone calls that later turn into passionate all-night lovemaking sessions. And day-long dates and four-day getaway weekends. Dinner at his mama's.

She knows that he works hard—recognizes that he doesn't just get that kind of dough handed to him by shirking his responsibilities and putting in half the time his ambitious coworkers put in. But she also knows that he tries his hardest to make it on time when she says she's cooking dinner, to make sure he finishes up his work before the weekend comes so that he can maximize his time with his intended, to avoid making plans on the evenings when friends and family request their presence at special events. He does these things because he knows they make her happy, and her happiness is important to him. So he puts in work.

The minute they walk down the aisle, though, brotherman loses it. She's his wife now, and that means that he doesn't have to be as careful with her feelings. She is supposed to, after all this good treatment during the courting and engagement phase, just suddenly understand that she's not riding shotgun anymore. No, she's in the backseat, see, and she's just supposed to accept that he's got to work late six days out of the week, and that his weekends have to be spent on the golf course with the boss if he wants to move up in the firm, and that her mama will get over it if he refuses to go to their house yet again when it's time to take the kids for a visit with the grandparents.

She is his wife now, see? She is supposed to simply understand.

But she doesn't. Because what it's come down to is that she's being taken for granted—and it's all being cloaked in the increasingly tired "I'm doing this for us, babe" thing. She didn't start tripping because he continued working that hectic NBA schedule, or kept working late trying to make partner at the firm, or putting in extra hours at the bakery to put a little extra in the bank for that new house they've dreamed about owning. She started tripping because he was no longer working hard to keep her happy.

The key word here is *happy*. This is all she wants. Oh, she wants him to keep working hard because she recognizes that every hard-worked hour is going to bring in another hard-earned dollar that will help keep the family stable. What she doesn't want, though, is for that dollar to come at the expense of the family. She'd much rather have him home with her and the kids at night than have an extra $500 in the bank come the end of the month. The money can be made anytime. But that family time lost?

Priceless.

She's upset because the man who worked so hard to keep her happy no longer appears to care if she's truly happy. He's simply doing that man thing—trying to one-up the next guy to prove how much bigger and better he is.

Unfortunately, this comes at the expense of his woman.

It's extremely hard to recover once she's set in her mind that he thinks the job is more important than her and the kids, because it doesn't ever seem that he plans on slowing down and hearing her side of the argument. How 'bout it:

Do men have the ability to slow down the work schedule and come to their senses when they see it's endangering their marriage?

From a Brother

I think what happens is the man recognizes there are problems at home, but by the time he figures out that the marriage is in a state of emergency and then decides what to do about it—which is much harder than it sounds—it's often too late to repair the damage.

As quiet as it's kept, many women in this situation are content to have partial marriages, partial husbands, partial dads—and the fully loaded Mercedes-Benz, Navigator, eight-bedroom mansion, wardrobe closet, shoe closet, and bank account. In other words, they let the big money buy their silence. They put on the happy face, smile when necessary, spread their legs when required, and stew inside about how much of an invisible asshole their husband is. Of course, if we're not hearing any complaints or seeing any obvious signs of hostility on the home front, we will continue to put in the crazy hours to make the crazy loot. We won't even grimace too much when the credit card bill comes every month.

Even if we know the wife isn't content and we see the storm brewing on the horizon, we have a really difficult time putting that zooming eight-cylinder high-performance engine that is our career into first gear and moving it over into the slow lane, watching all the other high-performance engines whiz by while we ferry the kids to soccer games and go to the mall with our wife. I'm not saying that spending quality time at home can't be enormously rewarding and fun, but much of it can also be mundane grunt work. We tell the senior partner too many times that we can't stay until 10 P.M. because it's the night of the parent-teacher conference, or the kid has a ballet recital, or the wife wanted us to stay home with the kids while she went out to dinner with her girlfriends, and we know he's going to start giving all those coveted assignments to someone else. We can't find a way to put the career on hold and let the hotshot with whom we've been competing for the past five years get all the glory and the even bigger bucks. So for a while we try to increase the number of hours in our day by forgoing sleep, or some equally necessary activity like meals and exercise. All that does is lead to illness, stress, and irreversible health problems. That's no answer either.

What we really need is for something to come along and give us some perspective. It could be an encounter with a disabled child to make us cherish our own healthy little tyke even more. Or an evening around a long-married couple with a special loving glow that tells us our priorities are in the wrong place. Sometimes a few memorable evenings with our lady—complete with the candlelight dinner, hand-holding, eye-gazing, and some absolutely terrific poontang—can help us acquire some perspective. But most of us have a hard time getting it on our own. That's what single-minded obsession means—we don't have the ability to direct our concentration to other things, like family and home, soon enough to spot trouble before it's already overtaking us.

And then there's the other factor that clouds the issue: the Silent Spender wife. The professional sports leagues are filled with these sistahs—and white girls—who don't even like spending a lot of time with their immature, basketball-bouncing, football-catching, baseball-hitting husbands. Many of them don't even like their husbands. (Can you say "gold digger"?) They don't want Face Time, they just want the credit card. We even heard from a few of them during the NBA lockout—women who started complaining about the play stoppage because they desperately wanted to get their husbands out of the house and on the road. To uphold their end of this marriage partnership, the men are all too happy to get the hell out of Dodge. What they do on the road, out of their lady's eyesight, is anybody's guess—and I'm sure you could give me some pretty good guesses—but that's not the wife's concern as long as he isn't out there making babies (though we know from the recent *Sports Illustrated* exposé on the explosion of illegitimate babies sired by professional athletes that too many of them can't even uphold this end of the bargain).

We all know the Silent Spenders are out there and we're not really sure if we have one of these until we're in a situation where she can reveal her true colors. Women aren't going to admit to being a Silent Spender before trouble arrives. You all are going to tell us that you need us to be home, you need us to be husbands in every sense of the word. Then a few years go by, the big money starts rolling in, and we keep looking around the corner to see if you're still content even though we rarely get home before 10. Whenever we look, all we continue to see are those pearly whites—letting us know that, despite your pronouncements to the contrary, what we have is a genuine Silent Spender. You go on spending and I keep on working.

A lot of women may not be ready to hear this, but you do have it within your control to snap your men out of the workaholic trance. What you need to do is remind your men why they fell in love with you in the first place. If you could put aside the anger and resentment and revisit that bright, cheery woman who used to smile back at you in the mirror, your husbands certainly would take notice. I'm not talking about a major transformation and I'm certainly not talking about plastic surgery or massive diets. I'm speaking of a change in outlook, of trying to find some way to purge the hostility that kicks up in your soul the second he walks into the door again after 11 P.M. Imagine his shock when he skulks in to find you smiling, welcoming him with open arms, sitting with him as he wolfs down the microwaved dinner, telling him how glad you are that he's finally home and maybe, on occasion, even slipping on the Victoria's Secret outfit that's been gathering dust in the back of your panty drawer. Of course, this only works if there's some love left for each other, if things haven't derailed so far off track that the only thing you'd want to do with those Victoria's Secret thongs is wrap them around his neck and watch his eyes bulge. But if there's a desire to get things back to the early days, you must remind each other of what the early days were like—the days when he still called you from work just to see how you were doing. If he's not going to take the initiative to bring you back there—and, unfortunately, you know that's unlikely—then the job falls on you.

Whose Word Wins— Your Spouse's or Your Family's?

From a Sistah

God, I love my parents.

I have been a writer for what seems to be my entire life, but still I struggle to find the words that can convey the awesome respect and admiration I have for these two people who raised me and loved me and taught me not only how to be a human being, but to be a good person. For over 30 years, I have watched them and listened to them and learned from them, trusted them and leaned on them, cried on their shoulders and let them convince me that it's okay to laugh again. They are the rocks that served as my foundation, the ones who crafted my morals, honed my sensibilities, pushed me to just be better.

I think they did a helluva job raising a helluva kid.

And I go out of my way to give them all the credit for making me the person I am today, because without them, I am almost sure I would neither be nor have anything.

This is what I'd always kept in mind when I was in high school and college—particularly when faced with the opportunity to do some stuff that I knew I shouldn't be doing. I'd always ask myself,

"What would my parents think if they found out about this?" before I did most anything questionable. Someone offering me weed? "What would the 'rents think?" Some guy trying to get me to sleep with him on the first date? "I know Daddy would be disappointed over this one—maybe I shouldn't." If I don't kill on this test, or get this new job, what will Mommy think? Better kick some serious ass.

Sure, some people may consider this odd—particularly men. Why, after all, would a grown woman be concerned about pleasing her parents?

Because it is the way we are raised. There is, you have to admit, something inherently different about the way parents raise their daughters as opposed to their sons. Boys are brought up tough, hard—taught to do it on their own because the world is a hard taskmaster and if you're not strong, it will eat you alive. Don't get me wrong—they are loved, but they are pushed to be men. Don't cry. Don't complain. Get up. Do it again until you get it right. Be a man, why don't you?

Girls? We're encouraged to depend—depend on Mommy and Daddy, on our men, on our friends. We are treated as feeble and weak, in constant need of assistance. It's okay if we mess up, because there will always be a shoulder to cry on, a bed to lie in, open arms to run to when the going gets hard.

You can imagine, then, how hard it is to give up that stability—that constant source of energy and support—to enter into a relationship where you're expected to make your own decisions. To be a grown-up. To run to someone else's arms. To be asked to go against all that you've ever known—or at least forgo running it past the parents before you jump into whatever with your mate. All of a sudden, three decades' worth of dependence is supposed to just disappear after the "I do."

I wholeheartedly argue that it's easier to dry up Niagara Falls.

Yet our men fully expect that once we enter into a relationship with them, this is exactly what we're to do: Forget about the parents and depend solely on him.

What a request.

I still find this to be, perhaps, one of the most challenging issues I face in my relationship with Nick, because my first inclination is always to run to Daddy and seek his advice on important topics like finances and careers, or to Mommy for advice on how to be a mommy and how to deal with problems that come up in our marriage. And this, I think, is okay to some extent—though I get the distinct feeling that my mate doesn't really appreciate it all that much.

He is, I assume, like any other man who wants to keep his household business in the house, rather than in the street, even if the street is full of people his woman loves.

This we do not get.

Why do men get offended when their women seek out support and advice from their families?

From a Brother

We don't expect you to cut off all contact with your folks; it's not like you get with us and you're suddenly consigned to the witness protection program. We even realize that you will talk to them about us; it's inevitable. But it is disconcerting to discover that not only do we have to keep our woman happy and sated and content, we have to do the same for another whole family out there that doesn't even live in our house.

I think when people commit to a man or a woman in marriage or in a serious relationship, we have a certain responsibility to protect our partner from the prying eyes and meddling opinions of family members. It's a necessity if our relationships are going to be allowed to trudge through those difficult times that are sure to come. What this protection means is that you present your partner in the best possible light whenever you can. I'm not talking about lying; I'm talking about putting his best foot forward in the same way that he would if he was the one talking to your folks.

If you don't do this, you create the following situation: The folks hear from you only when things are bad or you need advice, and they start believing that's the way things are all the time. That's what happened to a friend of mine. He was complaining about his wife on a regular basis to his sister and his mother, telling them how she was lazy and couldn't cook and had very little career ambition. Then one day he overheard his mother saying something derogatory to his sister about his wife, like they were sharing one of many jokes they'd shared at his wife's expense. And he noticed that they started treating her differently, too—they were a little colder and less respectful around her. He immediately gathered his mother and sister together and told them that he loved his wife immensely and there were so many wonderful things about her that he had no right complaining to them about a few of the things that bothered him when he was having a bad day or a bad week. It's like the way I used to feel when I covered the New York City school system as a reporter: If I'm going to keep writing a plethora of negative stories, it was my responsibility to balance it with some positive stories because otherwise the public got the incorrect impression that every school in the city was filled with violent, lazy, uncaring kids, which is the furthest thing from the truth. When we complain to our parents, we are giving them a small, inaccurate view of our relationship that will need to be balanced if we don't want them to start spitting at our mate's picture on their end table.

Balance means that you must call them up when things are going well and your mate is making you happy just to report that you are married to or living with a wonderful man. If things go well much more often than they go badly, you must tell them the good news much more often than the bad news to be fair and accurate. I am totally serious here; this is some important stuff. As Denene implied in her opening, your parents spend at least two decades looking out for your best interests, which in their mind surely includes keeping you away from bad, harmful men. We can't expect them to suddenly turn off this protective instinct when you get married. No, they will want to stay involved; they will offer advice, even if you didn't ask for it. Whenever they're around your man, they will start picking out all his negative qualities and telling themselves he's no good. That's what a reputation does—it changes the way people look at us. Dan Quayle is a dummy who can't spell *potato*—a decade later people still sit through his speeches waiting for the smallest screw-up so they can walk away with a Quayle story to tell people about their personal encounter with his stupidity. Bill Clinton is a philanderer—every time he's in the company of pretty women, people start snickering and nudging their friends because they're imagining what they think Clinton must be imagining.

When you complain about your man to your folks, what you are doing is building him a negative reputation in their minds. It could easily be a rep that's the furthest thing from what he's really like, but it will be too late to alter it—the damage will already have been done. Reps are hard as hell to shake. Just ask that girl y'all used to whisper about and call a tramp in high school. Or the dude in college who got accused of date rape and is having a real hard time finding female company. If you're going to spend the rest of your life with this man free from the destructive influences of the folks, you need to keep him reputation-free. You need to realize that if you get in the habit of running to Mom or Dad, you will not get in the habit of running to him to discuss whatever problems you might be having with him. Your parents only know what you tell them. If you tell them good things, that's what they will think. Tell them bad, and they think he's evil.

If your parents complain about your man, isn't it inevitable that you will internalize some of their complaints and believe them yourself?

From a Sistah

Sure. But then I'll come to my senses and remember that they are not living in my house, sleeping with my man, or walking in my shoes—and that it is me, ultimately, who has to decide whether this man is taking care of business the way I want my business to be taken care of.

I have a girlfriend whose husband recently decided to quit his job to pursue his first love—acting—full-time. He gave up a good job—he was an entertainment reporter—and an even better salary—$85,000—to get into a profession that is about as dependable as a crackhead with a grocery list and a $50 bill.

It was his dream, and his wife, though a bit concerned about how they would manage the mortgage, the car payments, and the kids' school tuition without a steady paycheck, supported his decision. They agreed that they would have to alter their spending habits and stick to a serious budget, and he agreed that if the acting thing didn't work out in a certain amount of time, he would find a steady-paying gig and turn his full-time pursuit of an acting career into a weekend hobby.

Needless to say, her 'rents were not happy. All kinds of things were going through their minds. Their daughter was going to be working, why couldn't he? Didn't this mean he would be a no-good, shiftless negro sitting up in the house while their daughter busted her behind to make ends meet? Who was going to take care of their grandchildren? Was he using their kid?

They made a point of letting their daughter know that they didn't approve of her husband's decision, and that they surely thought that he was shirking his responsibility to take care of his family. Every chance they got, they were downing him—calling him names, saying they didn't like him, encouraging their daughter to get out of what would soon turn into a troubled marriage.

My girlfriend, who'd fully supported her husband's decision with little reservation when he approached her about quitting his job, started turning on him when her parents started in on her. Soon, she was unsure of how she really felt about her husband's decision. Deep down, she, too, was worried about the kids and the mortgage and the tuition and the taxes, and she didn't want to carry the family's financial burden on her back—was afraid to, even. The more her parents spewed venom-filled words against her husband, the more my friend's relationship with her man became poisoned. She was tense; she was snapping at him; she, too, found herself thinking he was trifling.

And before she knew it, she blew.

Thing is, her husband was so very unsure about his decision, too, and though the last thing he wanted his wife to think was that he was lazy and unwilling to provide for his family, he knew that it would be inevitable that she would begin to feel this way anyway. And though he was defensive, he understood her delayed reaction.

What became of this? They talked. And talked some more. And deliberated. And deliberated some more. And, as husband and wife, they came to some serious conclusions and made even more serious decisions.

Before they knew it, the two of them were devising a more sound budget and action plan for their new, more exciting, but unsure life. And my girlfriend found herself defending her man to her parents, rather than listening to their snide comments and remarks. She had come to realize, after all, that the decisions she made with her husband were exactly that—decisions she and her husband made together. Though she respected her parents' input, she realized that she had to be the one to call the shots, because she was grown and had a family of her own, and the time had come for her to act like she was in charge of her own destiny.

She wasn't trying to hurt their feelings, but she did end up telling her parents to butt out—in a nice, respectful way, of course. And they did, recognizing, finally, that their little girl was grown.

It took them all a while, though, to find peace.

See, at first, she was damned if she did and damned if she didn't. When she followed their advice, there was trouble at home. When she didn't follow their advice, they hated her man even more because now, he was brainwashing all the sense out of their daughter. She was, quite simply, stuck.

And it's a hard row to hoe when you're stuck between your man and your 'rents. It means that holidays are never pleasant, phone conversations are curt, grandkids are stuck in the middle.

And the only one who can really make it right is the daughter.

This is not easy. But she knows that it needs to be done, because he is her husband. And no matter what her parents have to say about him, she is the one who married him and she is the one who has to be strong enough to keep that marriage going.

I would argue that most of us do this (eventually).

I would also argue that though the parents' criticisms of their daughter's mate may play some role in what she thinks about her man, it is she who ultimately decides whether she's going to let the negative assessments stick—on her own terms.

In the meantime, is there ever a time when a man can accept advice and help from his mate's family?

From a Brother

Yeah, if he goes to them for advice or help, then obviously he's ready to accept it. But if it's unsolicited, he may have a hard time with it.

Unsolicited advice or help from the woman's parents is rife with problems for several reasons that have everything to do with the peculiar state of maleness. First of all, as you may have noticed, we like to solve our problems on our own. Yeah, we know the female half of the planet has nothing but scorn for this particular male trait. We know that we'll infuriate you by refusing to ask for directions until we're staring at the Canadian border and wondering where we made the wrong turn on the way to Maryland. We know that you think it's childish and immature and silly for us to try to work out every problem by ourselves. But why not re-label this trait as independence and self-sufficiency and praise us for our pioneering spirit? Just think—if Columbus had stopped and asked the Native Americans how to get to India, they would have sent his lost ass back in the other direction and all the white people would have stayed in Europe and left the Africans in Africa. Okay, on second thought, maybe that's not such a good example. If Newton had asked his wife why that apple hit him on the head, she would have told him to stop daydreaming and take out the garbage and we still wouldn't understand what gravity is.

In fact, maybe you women could adopt a little of this pioneering spirit and work out more of your problems on your own instead of running to your girlfriends or your boyfriend or your mom and dad for help. Instead of viewing us as wrong-headed and stubborn for needing to do it on our own, we could turn the tables and call females needy and clingy and overly dependent for reaching out all the time instead of doing it on their own. As you can see, it's all a matter of perspective.

When we get unsolicited advice from your parents, it tells us two things: One, that they have somehow discovered that we have a problem that needs solving (wonder where they got that information?); and two, they don't think we're capable of solving it on our own. This realization will bother us a lot. The parents will justify their meddling by saying it is their daughter's well-being that they are seeking to protect. We do understand their concern, but that is also bothersome because it implies that we don't have enough concern for their daughter's well being. Certainly the guy who wants to pursue an acting career isn't interested in letting his wife starve or forcing her to slave away to support him. He's pursuing a dream on behalf of his whole family. If he succeeds, everyone will be the richer for it—literally and figuratively. How liberating and powerful a message he will send to his children in their formative years when they realize that their dad has managed to fashion a rewarding life with his God-given talent on his own terms, doing something he would do for free. They are taught that there's an infinite number of options out there besides the 9-to-5 trap, that the creative world is an exciting, satisfying place with the power to effect change and transform lives. I'd say those lessons are probably at least as valuable to a child as an Ivy League education. Probably more valuable. I'd venture to say the child of an artist—actor, writer, musician, painter, sculptor—is much more likely to want desperately to follow in his parents' footsteps than the offspring of a 9-to-5 toiler. In other words, if the daughter's husband wants to pursue that life, it's surely a worthwhile risk that could prove enormously beneficial in the long run to the daughter and her family.

All that being said, it's not impossible for us to recognize that your mother or father could be helpful in some cases. For instance, if you're acting like a spoiled knuckleheaded brat who doesn't seem to know what a marriage is all about, we might eventually look to your parents for help or advice. This is one circumstance when we might appreciate a little meddling. If we put you over our knee and spank you, we might get arrested (or you might shock us both by asking us to spank harder), but your parents are allowed to smack you all upside the head to bring you to your senses. We could accept that. We'd never do it ourselves, but we'd take pleasure in the benefits of the parent-smacking.

Ending It:
Does It Matter
Who Initiates the Breakup?

From a Sistah

I truly thought that he was the one.
Boy, was I dumb.

I'd met him through my best girlfriend's boyfriend. Actually, I'd seen his picture on my friend's wall and, proclaiming him the finest thing I'd ever seen (that week, at least), I asked my girl's guy to hook us up.

I should have known that it wasn't going to work; after a whirlwind winter/spring romance full of love letters, long telephone conversations, and sweet, tender—um, well, you get the picture—we both graduated from college and sort of went our separate ways, though temporarily. He went home and got a job working for a local community center there, while I moved to Albany, N.Y., for my first reporting gig.

And there I was, all alone, sleeping on the floor of a one-bedroom apartment with three windows—all facing a brick wall—toiling at a job with which I was unfamiliar, eating peanut butter and jelly sandwiches because I couldn't afford anything else, hours away from my family, friends, and man. There were two things that kept me going: One was knowing that this job, an internship with The Associated Press, would be over in three months; the other was knowing that I had a man who made me feel all warm and fuzzy inside.

Well, after three months, my job was finished and so was my relationship. I knew my three-month internship with the AP would come to an end. But my thing with that boy? Crashed harder than a rumbling truck against the hide of a deer in headlights.

Guess who was the deer?

Suddenly, his letters stopped coming. Suddenly, the phone stopped ringing. Suddenly, he was never home when I called, or even when I made the three-hour drive to visit him at his mom's house. Suddenly, his fingers seized up on his behind and he couldn't quite get them to dial my digits. Suddenly, I was all alone.

I never saw it coming.

It was my girlfriend's boyfriend who finally broke down and told me that this guy wasn't interested anymore—that he'd moved on and set his sights on some little girl who lived in their neighborhood. I was at my parents' house when I received the call, and all I can really remember is me hanging up the phone, walking into my parents' room, feigning to watch television, then bursting into tears, in front of my mom. And if any of you know my mom, you do not cry over some dumb little boy in front of her, unless you just really want to get called every dumb so-and-so in the book.

Didn't stop me, though.

"Girl, what's wrong with you," she said, kinda annoyed because my sobs were interrupting her television program and her sleep.

"What's wrong with me?" I practically yelled at her. The tears were intermingling with the snot and I had this crazy look on my face and my words were coming out at the top of my throat so it was really high-pitched, like that of a little girl who'd just skinned her knee and had gone running to Mommy to make it all better. "I don't understand!" I continued. "What's wrong with me?"

My mother had no idea what the hell was wrong with me, but she knew it was serious. I'm sure her first inclination was to crawl all in my behind for letting some boy get me all worked up like this—but, like a true mommy, she straightened up her face and asked me what was wrong. I explained that I was dropped like a bad habit and that I felt worthless and used and disrespected and disgusting and stupid because this guy broke up with me and everybody from around the way knew it but me. I didn't know what hurt worse—that I was without a boyfriend (again) or that I was embarrassed by the way he'd actually done the deed. At any rate, I was hurting, and had convinced myself that something was wrong with *me*, not him.

Mommy quite effectively explained to me that he was just a knot-headed boy who obviously didn't know what he had—a sweet, smart young woman who was going to make some man very happy and proud one day. Her words were a salve on my bruised heart, but it still hurt like hell, and it took me a long time to get my self-esteem back and figure out for myself that it was he who had the problem, not me. I'd done nothing wrong; I'd done nothing but love him and respect him and plan for our future together. He was the one who'd done wrong.

There isn't a single woman out there who hasn't gone through the same thing. Find him, like him, love him, get left—no doubt after he makes you feel like *you're* all wrong and *you* need help getting it together. The breakup is inevitably nasty, ugly, rude—and until we grow up, we're going to think it was something that we did to make him go away.

Our womanhood is shattered.

We don't know how to deal.

And it takes a long, long time before we can move on—before we can present our bruised hearts to the next guy without thinking he's going to stomp all over it, too. In essence, it's pretty hard to make that person who broke up with us official black history.

Does it work that way for brothers?

If I break up with you, would it destroy the delicate balance that is your manhood?

From a Brother

To be honest, I'm not so sure we would internalize it to that extent after just three months of a relationship, but we certainly can relate to the pain. Getting dumped is a rejection, plain and simple, a comment by another person on your worth, your attractiveness, your desirability. It's not nice to be told that somebody else is better than you—or that you're not good enough, even if there is nobody else.

This may not have been the case in Denene's situation, but I have often felt—and other guys have told me they have felt the same way—that women force men into ending bad relationships so that we can forever be known to her and her friends as Dickhead. She will twist herself into a pretzel to avoid bringing down the hammer herself, even if she knows that she'd rather spend an evening chatting with Mike Tyson than five minutes with us. It's almost as if the women have this desperate need to be able to blame the man once it comes crashing down. If she initiated the breakup herself, what could she tell her friends?

So when we actually find ourselves on the receiving end of a breakup speech or telephone call or E-mail (damn, that would be cold), we will be shocked. And we will conclude that we must have been pretty damn awful for the girl to go ahead and initiate the breakup herself. We'd know that pushing her into the breakup speech is about as easy as forcing her to leave the mall after a half hour. We'd start thinking that she must think we're a real jerk. But then you know what would happen?

We'd go outside. We'd walk by a lot of pretty girls. Some of them may even know us and might have been waiting for our terrible relationship with so-and-so to come to an end. They might proceed to smile up in our face. We will smile back in theirs. By the end of the day, we might even have a few phone numbers. Now, what were you asking me about my manhood?

Even if I was terminally in love with my ex, I'm still going to be able to drown my sorrows pretty quickly in Tanisha's C cups or Lisa's big ol' booty. It certainly will mean that the breakup will have no impact on my views of my manhood. None. In fact, if my relationship with my ex had deteriorated to the point where she was insulting my manhood, it's gonna feel pretty good to be around somebody who even offers to slob my knob once in a while—or, heaven forbid, get me a glass of soda when she goes to the kitchen.

I'm not saying that we will necessarily be proposing to any of these new women. As a matter of fact, these new women may find themselves replaced by an even newer woman every few weeks or so in a dizzying display of playahood. We may seek this bounty of booty as a way to force ourselves to forget what we had and lost. But as long as the booty keeps coming and it is, indeed, bountiful, we eventually will find ourselves healed. And our manhood will be anything but destroyed. Might be tired, but not destroyed.

If we break it off—even if you know it wasn't working—why do you remain so bitter for so long?

From a Sistah

Because half the time, there was no indication that anything was wrong with the relationship—until one day, out of the clear blue sky, your words hit us like a left hook: "Things, um, just aren't working out," you'll say as you're walking out the door, never to be heard from again. Or, worse yet, you won't even bother telling us; we'll find out you're not ours anymore when you suddenly stop calling and coming around, or we hear her voice on the other end of the line, telling us that you are no longer ours. All we know is that our heart is just broken and we feel awful and we need to do something to make ourselves feel better and the way to do that is to get back at that man as best we can—and if being bitter and nasty and evil to him and any other man makes us feel just a little better, then you better watch out because you're going to have to face the wrath.

I can soundly say that I haven't been on the receiving end of a breakup too many times, but the few times that it did happen, it hurt like hell. And I know that I wanted to do whatever I could to get back at him, short of stabbing him and spending the rest of my life in prison.

My ex, Leslie, can tell you. We'd been dating for, oh, about seven months or so and everything was smooth daddy—or so I thought. We spent most of our free time together—stayed at each other's apartments, cooked for each other, shopped together, loved each other. Well, at least we said it to each other, and I know, at least, that I meant it. I was sure he did, too, until one evening, he took just a little bit longer than usual getting home from work. By the time he finally got to my house, dinner was cold—but I didn't really sweat it. We ate, and then, like we usually did, we sat on the couch to talk. Everything, I was confident, was just fine.

"Um, I have to tell you something," he said.

"What's up," I said, matter-of-factly, not really paying much attention to the tension in his voice.

"I want us to be friends," he said.

My mouth dropped. My eyes narrowed. My brow furled. My first inclination was to curse his ass out. I'm sure I did. Then I did the strangest thing: I left him sitting on the couch while I retreated to the bathroom to, get this, wash my hair. Wash my hair, y'all. In hindsight, I can truly say that I did this because I needed to just get away from him, from his face, his voice, the words. I was embarrassed—humiliated, even—and the only thing I could think to do at the time was to get the hell out of that living room and do something mindless to take my mind off the fact that I was just dumped like yesterday's trash. Except trash, if it had the processes to think, would understand said dumping. I simply did not.

And instead of trying to understand, I decided in my mind that I was going to do everything within my power to make him feel like five pounds of crap stuffed into a three-pound bag. So when he tried desperately to call the house to say hi, or hold a conversation with me at work (we worked in the same building), I would simply forgo returning his phone calls or refuse to speak to him in the hallways, making sure that everyone within eye- and ear-shot knew I was dissing the mess out of him. He became my arch enemy. I treated him like he stole from my mama.

None of this really made me feel better in the long run. But for the short term, it felt damn good. Because I wanted to hurt him like he hurt me—and the only way that that could happen was for me to be as mean and evil and nasty and bitter toward him as possible.

See, this is what makes sense. It is purely a sistah reaction—shoot, a human reaction. If someone hurts you or someone you love, you want to get back at them—I don't care how forgiving a heart you *think* you have. Someone robs you? You report it to the police and, if they catch the bastard, you take him to court—hope he gets a stiff prison sentence. Someone hits your car? You report him to the insurance company and sue him for all he's got, because he jacked up your ride. Someone does something to compromise your integrity at the job—in front of the boss? You know what to do. The first time you have the opportunity, you stab that person in his professional back, in front of the boss, so that person knows not to mess with you ever again.

Same thing with the man who breaks up with you. You get him back any way you can, and you make sure that it hurts—or that, at the very least, it makes you feel hella better than you did when he told you to beat it.

Sure, there are some who will argue that they respond to such actions in a Christian way, and I certainly admire those with that kind of will. But realistically? Revenge is the way to go for a whole lot of us. Bitterness is usually mixed all up in it.

Eventually, she will learn to get over it, as I did with Leslie. One day, I just decided that it just took too much out of me to be mean to him—particularly since I'd moved on and found someone special for myself. I no longer wanted him. I no longer needed him. My ripped heart was being darned by a helluva man who was going out of his way to love me and make me feel loved. And I loved him back—hard, strong.

And now, I thank God that Leslie just wanted to be friends, because he freed me up to find true love, in the arms of my Nick.

This is the way it usually works for women: They get cut loose, they cut up, they meet someone new, they convince themselves that this guy won't do the same thing the last guy did, and they fall in love, hoping that this time, it will work out. And poof! the bitterness disappears.

If you use other women to drown the sorrow of a breakup, does that mean we should avoid a man who has recently gotten out of a serious relationship if we don't want to be used and discarded?

From a Brother

If only it were that simple to avoid being used and discarded. The problem is, virtually every single adult male has recently gotten out of a serious relationship. If the man hasn't recently gotten out of a serious relationship, then he probably has some issues that'd make you want to avoid him just like all the other women have. So women who pledge that they will never be in a "rebound" relationship will be relegated to choosing from the runts of the litter.

We know women are aware of the Poontang Prescription for breakup recovery. It's almost become a cliché in our society. If a doctor wrote out the Poontang Prescription, it would say something like "take as much as possible, early during the morning's warm salute of the rising sun and into the night's brooding heat, feeding that longing that throbs in your soul until the heartache recedes to a distant memory." Or maybe: "Get ass and lots of it."

You get the idea.

Women have plenty of models to instruct them that a "rebound woman" isn't in the most enviable position. Our society even has the stereotype of the divorced man, drowning whatever sorrow he may be feeling in an array of bimbos and fast cars. He is laughable and he is pitiable, but he is also instructive. Like Donald Trump. It doesn't please me to use him as a positive example of anything concerning men—like anyone else, my blood curdles at the sight of his annoyingly smug mug, even when he's without a new imitation supermodel on his arm—but his life is a caricatured example of my point. The Donald doesn't sit around and wonder if he's still worthy or desirable after a relationship ends—he goes out there and quickly scoops up another trophy, seemingly never taking the time for introspection or self-reflection. One has to wonder if there has ever been a moment of self-reflection in Donald's life—at least more than would be necessary to call up the next gossip columnist to tell her how badly he feels about his last break-up. (Though I was pleased last year to see that Donald had the self-awareness to laugh at himself and recognize the ridiculousness of his public image when he appeared in a television commercial that showed him participating in an art class to meet babes.)

Most of us, probably even Donald, are capable of recognizing when that special Miss walks into our lives. The Poontang Prescription doesn't induce blindness—it just puts us on a single-minded quest to drown our sorrows in a sea of succulent lady nectar. I've known plenty of men who were passionate about their quest for as much as they could get as often as they could get it. They hit all the right clubs, the outdoor jazz concerts, the classier street fairs, anywhere they knew there'd be plenty of poontang. It became their avocation. It might have started out as a way to pave over the hurt from the crumbled relationship, but eventually that old girlfriend or wife was a distant memory. Now, they were just dogs without a leash. Then one day they got zapped. SHE walked into their lives and the quest was over, the doggin' long forgotten.

The point is this: There's no need to avoid us just because we recently got kicked to the curb by somebody else. If you were meant to be the one that we set our eyes on first thing every morning, then we'll find a way to sweep all our baggage aside and leave some room in our hearts for love to sprout. It may be a little scary at first for all parties concerned when we realize what's happening—i.e., we may have a few moments of temporary insanity when we run from your house in full bellow as we attempt to get away from that fluttering in our hearts—but we'll soon come to our senses because we won't want to lose you. A man's primary concern after a breakup is the avoidance of all relationship pain for as long as he can stave it off. That's why we seek only the casual encounter, because we know it won't have the likelihood of ending up with us sobbing in a six-pack of Heineken. The casual woman decides she doesn't want to have anything to do with us, we figure: no harm, no foul. But as long as we're getting out there and leaving ourselves open to meeting new ladies, there's always the probability that we will one day be zapped again. We'll know it might end up in more pain, but we'll peek at this new lady and know she's worth the risk.

Part III

Respect

Respect

13

Hello?: Why Isn't He Listening to Me?

From a Sistah

I once dated this guy who was about as conversationally engaging as a gurgling four-month-old baby. No, hold up—let me correct that. At least the baby would babble back every once in a while—kick you a smile here and there to let you know that she is actually intrigued by your efforts to engage her.

But not Eugene (yes, I changed his name to protect him—but I don't know why. It's not like he deserves even this small piece of respect.). Eugene was perfectly content sitting in a room with me for hours without really saying much of anything—and even when he did open his mouth, it would usually be to say something smart-ass or trite. I'd read an interesting story in the *New York Times* and offer up my opinion on the subject, he'd nod and continue doing whatever it was that he was doing (usually, that would be staring at the television screen at a ball game, one hand on the remote, the other either wrapped around a beer or scratching somewhere below his belt). I'd tell him a funny story about one of my goofy girlfriends and her antics at one of our off-the-wall party nights, and he'd respond by telling me that my girls were stupid and continue doing whatever it was that he was doing (yup—ball game, remote, beer, scratching). One time, I told him I could cook really well—and he looked up from the screen and bet me that I couldn't cook better than his mama. Then he turned back to the ball game, the remote, the beer, and the scratching.

Didn't take me long to figure out that this person was not the man for me. First of all, any man who tells me I can't cook better than his mama needs to get dropped. Even if I can't cook as well as his mama, be a gentleman and at least pretend like I'm a good damn cook. Dummy.

Anyway, I'm a talkative kinda gal—need to discuss ideas, ponder issues, hear opinions. It's what keeps me alive, the idea that the world is always moving and evolving and that I'm a part of it. To me, talking is exercise for the brain—a way for me to keep up with the world, to make my mark in it. Can't stand no bump on the log who can't keep up.

Needless to say, Eugene got dropped.

And then came Cole. He was a little better. At least he didn't scratch while he was watching the ball game. But he still wasn't really interested in what I had to say. It was like talking to a brick wall with this guy—hardly any conversational engagement whatsoever. Oh, he'd talk every once in a while, but only when it was something that he brought up, which was rare. And when I'd start the topic of conversation, he'd pretend that he was interested for exactly 90 seconds, then do something to try to shut me up, like rudely find something else to do outside of the room where we were talking, or, even worse, try to kiss or caress me—you know, get something going.

The latter would certainly piss me off, because it made me feel used, like I was just there for his sexual pleasure.

I can't say that every man I've ever dated is as extreme as Eugene and Cole, but I can honestly attest to the fact that most of the men I'd been involved with just weren't engaging. I mean, I could go to work and talk with my girlfriend Christena the entire day, then go home, get on the phone, and talk some more. Then get up and do it all over again the next day—without once talking about the same thing. Granted, a substantial part of our conversation is gossip, jokes, and innuendo, but there is substance to what we discuss, too—our hopes, our dreams, our fears, our nightmares. There is no subject that goes unturned between girlfriends. Whether we agree or disagree on the issues, we respect each other's opinions and aren't afraid to explore each other's minds. And somehow, the conversation is always fresh.

One of the most attractive things about Nick—besides those juicy lips, those pretty brown eyes, that beard, and that bod (um, okay, I'm probably oversharing)—was and is his ability to hold his end of a conversation. One of the coolest things about our relationship is our ability to talk to each other about anything. It's been like this from the beginning. I think because we were friends for so long, we felt comfortable enough around one another to share our thoughts and feelings without being judgmental. The added bonus here is that Nick is so incredibly smart that I always feel like I'm learning something from him, too—so I look forward to our discussions about the latest educational issues, or the hot political topics of the day, or our kids and family, or even the difference between fried chicken from Popeye's and Kentucky Fried. Doesn't matter what it is we're talking about—I always feel like the conversation is worth it.

With other men, it just never felt this way. I always got the feeling that what I had to say was not worth listening to. It was a serious self-esteem dropper to have my mate dismiss my thoughts.

My girlfriends complain of the same thing—that the guys they date just aren't interested in talking to them. It's the weirdest thing to us; we seriously don't get it.

Why do guys avoid conversation—and, above all else, appear to not really care about what we women have to say?

From a Brother

The guys who avoid conversation on meaty, worldly matters are probably brothers who don't have anything to say—like the ex dummies described above. But the guys who do have something intelligent to contribute and don't mind participating in good conversation often complain to me that they have a hard time finding women who can talk about anything interesting.

If you want proof that most brothers don't mind at all talking about things that interest them, just drop into a barbershop on a Saturday afternoon—or any day of the week, for that matter. Barbershop conversation, while it may often begin and end on topics that revolve around sports, usually seems to have a life of its own. Brothers come in, sit down, hear what's being discussed, and within five minutes are drawn into heated discussion and disagreement with someone who might be a total stranger. The barbers usually act as the moderators and referees, keeping the debate moving along if it bogs down too much, scolding brothers who get out of line or start using inappropriate language ('cause you can be sure there's some little boy in the corner waiting for a cut with his Dumbo ears taking it all in), and giving props to anyone who has constructed a particularly airtight argument. Aside from sports, the other big topics are women, racism, and work. Barbershop conversation on these four topics can go on for hours with barely a pause, with new players coming in to replace those who leave, new points of view constantly being added to the mix. Yeah, men certainly can talk—about things they want to talk about.

That's where women come in. Ironically, one of the topics that recently got an airing at Mahir's, my Montclair barbershop, was the lack of conversational skills that brothers are finding among the females these days. Guys still on the dating scene are saying that a whole lot of these ladies in their twenties have absolutely nothing to say and can't hang at all when the brothers try to engage them in real conversation. Real conversation means we're talking about something other than your latest dilemma over which way to style your hair or what color fingernail polish to apply or what kind of blouse would best match those new black capri pants you just bought. For a lot of women, this is the kind of stuff they expect us to be thrilled to talk about with them. They throw this at us in never-ending streams and get angry when our response is less than enthusiastic.

Brothers with a head on their shoulders would pay good money to find a woman who can participate in real conversation. It's always been one of the things that I've been especially attracted to—smart women with something to say. Yeah, of course I want them to be fine, too—in fact, the combination of brains and beauty is the final stop in sexiness for me. There's nothing more thrilling than stumbling across a woman who has all those qualities in abundance and with whom you never want to stop talking.

We're not always going to be interested in everything that our women are interested in. We are not a replacement girlfriend, to fill in when your girl's phone number is busy and you just have to talk about that sale you discovered at Lord & Taylor. We might be able to take a few minutes of sale talk—enough to share your joy—but after that we will get eye glaze and want to be somewhere else. If you think this is cruel or unfeeling on our part, let us try out an experiment on you. Indulge us for a week. When we read the sports pages and watch games on TV, we will come to you and talk out all our reactions to whatever we see and read that gets us going. The Yankees trade David Wells for Roger Clemens—ohmy-God! That's huge! We need at least 45 minutes to an hour to get through the implications of that and our feelings about it. That's how long we'd talk about it in the barbershop or with one of our sports-crazed friends. The Lakers acquire Dennis Rodman? You know we're going to need an hour for that one. How 'bout Barry Sanders's retirement? You might as well stay home from work today, baby, 'cause I need about three or four hours of your undivided attention.

If you try this experiment and you find yourself getting eye glaze five minutes into every conversation with your enthusiastic mate, you might understand our position. It's not that we love you any less if we don't get as excited about the same things you do. We just aren't that interested, that's all. That shouldn't be construed as the end of the world.

If we aren't in the mood to talk, wouldn't it make you feel even worse if we came out and told you that—rather than fake it and half listen?

From a Sistah

There is absolutely nothing worse than trying to hold a conversation with someone who's barely paying attention to what you have to say. I'd rather go in the room and talk to my damn self than be denigrated by a person who obviously doesn't mind me wasting my breath. Besides, if he came out and told me he didn't want to talk, at least I could feel like I got some conversation. He will have told me how he feels—certainly a breakthrough in and of itself.

Imagine yourself walking into an interview—on your best behavior, got on your good suit, nice shoes, slamming résumé in hand. You're excited about the prospect of getting this job. You want to impress the interviewer—dazzle him with your wit and intelligence. He asks you a dumb question, something like what is your biggest weakness, and you, having anticipated said dumb question, offer up a serious pearl of an answer.

Except this guy isn't really listening to you.

Oh, he's looking at you, all right. But it's that blank, "I'm looking right through you" stare—you know, the one where if you moved your head just a little bit to the right, he'd be staring at the wall behind you and, even worse, wouldn't have even realized he'd been exposed. Because his mind will have been on something else, like getting his clothes out of the dry cleaner by tomorrow morning so that he can pack tomorrow night for the trip he's going to take that following morning, where he'll give a speech on the migration of Canadian geese. It would be clear to you that you could tell him you like to come into work first thing in the morning to masturbate to the sound of the coffeemaker and he wouldn't have even heard you—would have kept right on nodding and saying, "uh-huh" every seven words or so, just to make it appear he's listening to you.

This is jacked up, because this interviewer decided somewhere between the time you walked in the door and the time you sat down that you weren't worth his attention—that you didn't deserve the job, really, because you weren't all that impressive. And you will automatically feel like crap because you will have no idea what you did wrong, and your mind will begin to race. "Did he not read my résumé? Does he think I'm not qualified for the job? Is he racist? Probably going to hire some white boy he met on the golf course— the bastard." And you will leave the office dejected, convinced that his inattention was a surefire sign that you're not going to get the gig.

Well, the same thing goes when our man half listens to what we have to say and fakes his way through a conversation. We pretty much start assuming that he really doesn't like us—that he could care less about the things that we like and dislike, what we think, and how we respond to certain situations and people. His lack of a verbal response is taken as a sign that something is wrong in the relationship, because we just aren't communicating.

In this, there is no gratification for me. I am talking to myself. And while I don't mind talking to myself every once in a while— it keeps me sane, really—I like to do that alone, not in someone else's company. When I'm talking to someone, I expect a conversation from that person, not a blank stare, a half-nod, and an "uh-huh." Just tell me you don't want to be bothered right now, and I'll find something else to do. It's really not that big of a deal.

But you better choose your "I don't feel like being bothered right now"s carefully—because if I start to hear that every time I try to strike up a convo, I'm going to assume that you're really not interested in me. And I might be inclined to find someone who is.

Would men rather we women clam up and not talk to them?

From a Brother

No, we are not trying to make you clam up. We just want you to understand that just because you're interested in something doesn't mean that we are, too.

It's funny to me that women seem to think we have a special relationship with silence, that we cherish it so thoroughly that when we get together with our boys we all sit around and say nothing, worshipping our beloved peace and quiet. That's not true at all. When we get together with our boys, we have plenty to talk about. We can talk into the morning's wee hours, just like you ladies can with your girls. What's the difference here? When we talk with our boys, we are going to make sure we choose topics of mutual interest—like women and sports and racism and work. Sometimes when we're out with the boys we even ask ourselves before raising a topic whether it would be something that the other parties would want to talk about. If we choose incorrectly and the other person or persons look bored, we don't get upset at them. We conclude that we chose something that doesn't interest them so we better hurry up and change the subject. Notice the subtle difference in our response and yours—we take the blame for their lack of interest, we don't blame them for it. And we certainly don't conclude that something must be wrong with our friendship because he's bored with this particular topic.

Some guys even develop a reputation for introducing boring topics that have no point. When I was in college one of my friends was notorious for embarking on long, pointless stories that seemed to have no end. He'd seem to get stuck in the middle of his stories and forget why he even started it. Needless to say, we didn't have a lot of patience with him or his stories. When he was about to begin one, we'd practically require him to first give us an executive summary listing the story's purpose, its topic, and its duration. If he failed on these points, we'd tell him to keep quiet. This may sound mean but he didn't seem to mind. After all, we were his buddies.

We don't like to hear people—man, woman, or child—talk just to hear themselves talk. People who are in love with the sound of their own voice. People who seem to have an aversion to silence, feeling like they need to fill up any empty space with sound, even if it's pointless sound. What we feel like we sometimes get from our women is chatter—incessant words spewed out in unending streams about nothing in particular.

Over time, I've developed the kind of relationship with my younger sister Angelou that permits us to be brutally honest with each other when it comes to conversation. If I'm telling her a story or an anecdote that she's not interested in, she'll quickly tell me—and enjoy doing so. I will do the same thing with her. So when we talk to each other, we are constantly on guard to avoid the boredom territory because we know once we land there we will instantly get dissed by the other person. It's entertaining, but it's also instructive. It's our tacit acknowledgment to each other that the other person can't come with something weak that wastes our time. The story and the conversation has to have meaning, a reason for being. Otherwise she's going to tell me about it, or I will tell her. Our feelings never get hurt because we know we love each other and it's partly in fun. I'd bet a lot of guys would love to have a similar relationship with their mates, where they could raise their hand and let her know in an instant that she has veered into boredom territory. Denene says women wouldn't mind hearing this on occasion from their men, but I have a hard time believing that one. Maybe I'll try it out on her and see what she does. If I'm missing an eye the next time y'all see me, you'll know what happened.

Whose Career
Is More Important?

From a Sistah

I know you guys are going to hate the reference, but y'all remember what happened to Bernadine in Terry McMillan's *Waiting to Exhale*, right? She put aside her lifelong dream to open her own business and yielded to her husband's wishes—helped him finish school, worked as his secretary to help get his company up and running, bore his babies, kept his house clean, and dedicated the other two minutes of the time she had left to making *him* happy.

And what did she get for it?

He left her for a white girl. And tried to hide all the money she had helped him make. And all she was left with was a house she couldn't afford and a serious dream deferred.

True, *Waiting to Exhale* was a piece of fiction, but the reason it did so incredibly well was that we women could identify with its themes of friendship, disappointments, lost and found love, and used love. We all knew Savannah's Lionel, we all were as stupid at that love thing as Robin, we all battled Gloria's self-esteem issues. And though some of us may not have gone through exactly what

Bernadine went through, we sistahs could certainly understand what it meant for her to haul all her dreams to the curb to make some serious room for his goals—no matter how lofty or seemingly unattainable they may have been.

It is what we've all been conditioned to do. We grew up watching our mamas do what had to be done to support our daddy's decisions—she moved clear across the country with him when he really wanted that job, went without a few necessities when he took a job that wasn't paying quite enough, even went out and got a job when he was out of work. And just as Mom made sacrifices to help Dad do what he wanted to do, we learned that a necessary part of a grown-up relationship with a man is understanding that a real woman—a good companion or wife—supports his every move, because he is the man and his decisions, somehow, weigh more in the relationship, no matter how hard we try to pretend that things are equal.

Part of this, I think, has to do purely with reproduction. This may sound, well, Neanderthalish, but it is always at the back of our minds: What will happen if we get pregnant? If the two of us have salaries that sustain a certain lifestyle, there's always the chance that pregnancy and child-rearing will eliminate one of the paychecks, namely ours. So we have to make sure he's at the top of his game—make sure that he has enough dough to get us and the babies through the lean times. If that means we need to support his moving the family from New York to the suburbs of Washington, D.C., for a better-paying job and cheaper living expenses, we bone up to it because we know that staying at a less lucrative job and paying that higher rent would seriously impair our finances at our most vulnerable time—while we're trying to raise a family.

An even larger part of our supporting his career goals is purely romantic. I mean, think about it: We stick by him during law school or med school or that MBA program or his ball-playing college years because we know that at the end of the rainbow is our ring and title—Mrs. Lawyer, Mrs. Physician, Mrs. Wall St., Mrs. NBA. We figure if we stick it out with him long enough, he'll understand that we were always in his corner, even in the leanest of times, and that we deserve him, not the hootchie who's looking to get into his wallet now that he has the title and the money. "I was there with you from the beginning, baby—when you had neither a pot to piss in nor a window to throw it out of," we'll gently remind him. Our reward will be the right to help him spend it.

But there will come a time when we will feel like we've put in our time. We will want desperately to do something for ourselves—to feel like we've not only made a significant contribution to our household, but that we are doing what we've always dreamed of doing. It could be as simple as taking that extra course at the local college, or as complicated as quitting our job to go into business on our own.

Regardless of what it is, all too often, we end up like Bernadine—worn out from putting our all into our man, only to have our own dreams unrealized because we invested too much in his. Bernadine's delicious payback, of course, was that in the divorce, she won enough of his money to pay her mortgage, support her kids, and start her own business. But her husband had to have his ass dragged through court for her to get it.

Sometimes, I think that's what we all need to do to brothers in order to get the chance to pursue our ambitions. Rarely does the encouragement come from you all for us to pursue that extra degree, to go for the better position, to quit the job and strike out on our own. Oh, there are some men who will back their women up, but I'd venture to say that there are too many brothers out there who would feel threatened by the idea of their woman forging ahead with career goals that could make her earning power equal or better than his.

So he'll go out of his way to continue his career aspirations—asking her to put hers on hold until he makes "just one more dollar, baby, please?" He'll put on those puppy dog eyes and turn his lips down at the corners—make himself look pathetic, yet worthy. "Could you do this for me, for us—for the kids?" And before you know it, another year has gone by with our personal dreams as stagnant as the Louisiana Bayou.

This is just my humble opinion. Perhaps you can help me here: **Why do men always put their career goals ahead of their women's career goals?**

From a Brother

I think you did a good job of answering this question: Because we've all been taught that it's supposed to happen that way—and we men have the ultimate responsibility of ensuring that our family is supported. We know that if our wife and kids are out there on the line at the soup kitchen, and we're an able-bodied individual who still possesses his mental faculties, society will look for us when they come with the bucket of tar and the feathers. If we get evicted from our apartment or the bank forecloses on our house, it is us that your family and friends will come after with a baseball bat. They'll know that you are just as educated and accomplished as us, but they still view it as our responsibility to fend for family.

So we usually just assume that it is in everyone's best interest if we make it as far in our careers as we possibly can. We are treated as the breadwinner; we have to go on out there and win that bread. Of course, this is the traditional approach to the question, and it fits best in the traditional relationship where the man is seen by both himself and his wife as the primary wage-earner—and anything she makes is just gravy. Admittedly, the number of these kinds of relationships is dwindling, so for most of us, this old formula needs some substantial updating before we can apply it to our own relationships.

Men who become involved with talented, ambitious women in the new millennium know in the back of their minds that there may come a day when someone has to make a tough decision about whose career takes priority. It can be a painful matter to confront and most couples consequently avoid it as long as possible, kinda hoping it will go away. And then there it is, sitting in front of them like a big stinking gorilla, demanding that they deal with it or watch him wreck the place. I've seen this career stuff destroy too many marriages for couples to wait until the last minute to deal with it. Two very dear friends of mine saw their marriage crumble because they didn't pay enough attention to it and were instead too focused on career satisfaction. He had been doing quite well as an attorney, with a position that required him to travel around the world at a moment's notice. It was exciting stuff and he was good at it. His wife wasn't doing quite so well. She just couldn't seem to find that perfect job that she was destined to do, as he had. She knew she liked working in politics, but the big question was in what capacity. Then a great opportunity came along for her to work on another continent doing political organizing. The time frame was supposed to be about three months, which is a long time to be away from your spouse. The strain was going to be difficult, even if they stayed in close communication during her time away. But they didn't. And, to no one's surprise, she absolutely loved what she was doing. She was asked to extend her stay for another six months and she accepted. That's nine months away from her husband. Nine months is a long time, damn near a year that they had a marriage in name only. And by the time she came back, they didn't even have that. Too much time and space had eaten away at the love, the passion, the longings. There was little left for them to work with. The marriage quietly ended—no fights, no threats, apparently not even anger. It just kind of fizzled out. They had allowed the careers to thrive at the expense of the relationships, and they had had little communication in the process. They just assumed everything would be okay.

This issue is complicated because even if the man or the woman really believes his or her career should take priority, he's going to have a difficult time coming right out and saying it. And if the relationship stops him from taking a treasured job or promotion, he's going to harbor some resentment that will reemerge at the least opportune time. It's hard to turn this thought into action, but no one's career should be more important than the marriage. If things haven't yet proceeded to the marriage stage, then the obstacles preventing you from taking that fantastic job in another city are lower, more easily surmounted. But once you've exchanged vows, things get real dicey. Job offers come and go—marriages shouldn't.

You cite *Waiting to Exhale* as an example of a woman putting her dreams aside for her husband's career, but in most real-life scenarios the husband doesn't tell his wife that she can't pursue her dreams. Yeah, he may have a high-powered career that brings home a lot of loot and doesn't require her to work, but most men in this day and age aren't going to open their mouths and tell their women they have to stay at home—even if that's what they believe. We live in an age of ambition, where the man and the woman, the husband and the wife, the father and the mother, are both allowed and even expected to fulfill their long-held ambitions to make themselves happy. Every women's magazine article at some point winds its way to the one pervasive theme: how to be happy. Men know this—we have access to *Oprah* and *Ladies' Home Journal*. We know how much of a turd we would be in her mind if we took actual steps to prevent her from reaching for that happiness. And we know how quickly we'd be sending the relationship into the danger zone. So unless we're looking to get out, we shut up.

If it came time to make a decision as to whose career takes priority, how would we decide?

From a Sistah

I guess the obvious answer would be to support the career choice that would take the least amount of time to achieve, and, at the same time, would net the highest earnings. But the obvious answer isn't always the best answer, particularly in this case, because passion can far outweigh any timetables and earnings potential. Should one person's dream go deferred because it won't net as much as the other's? I think not. I'd keep my eye on the passion—heed the call for my mate's need to fly.

I knew back in February 1999 that I'd have to gird myself for a huge change when I encouraged Nick to leave his reporting job with the *Star-Ledger* to pursue his book-writing passion full-time. Things just weren't working out, you know? Here was this respectable education writer—one of the most brilliant in the business—and he was about to be relegated to a do-nothing job in the paper's City Hall bureau. See, the boss had figured that my baby had burnt himself out on his education beat and that he needed a change.

Needless to say, the boss was wrong. Both Nick and I knew it was more a demotion than anything, and that his career would stall for sure if he was caught toiling in the paper's all-but-irrelevant local political pages.

So I advised him to quit.

And he did.

And I kicked myself in my own ass for a good four months because I'd convinced myself that the uncertainty of fiction-writing was going to cause my then-unborn child to go without. I mean, I was about to go on maternity leave, and that meant that I was going to be going without a paycheck for as long as I decided to stay home with my child. And here I was, encouraging my husband to throw away a steady income for the unstable full-time writer's life, replete with book deals gone awry and unsure book advances. I had, at some point, worked myself up into such a panic that we were going to go broke and starve that I'd actually told him I wanted him to go back to work.

I know this had to hurt his feelings, because here was his encouraging wife telling him, in essence, that she would no longer support his goal to become a best-selling author.

I admit it: I was delusional. I chalk it up to the hormones. Because it has been almost a year and we are doing just fine. Book deals are pouring in. Our money isn't funny. Our child is well fed, well dressed, and extremely bright and happy. Life couldn't be better.

I'll have to admit that it took me a minute to see the big picture, but I'd like to think that I eventually came back to my senses because I knew that my baby's dreams were so very important to him. All his life, all he's wanted to do was to go to a bookstore and see his name on a book on a bookshelf there. And it has come to pass. My baby needed to fly, and I didn't clip his wings.

See what I mean by the passion?

Of course, the second part to making the decision as to whose career goals are more important is the promise that the one who gets to pursue his dreams first recognizes that eventually, his mate will have to have her turn. This means that in a reasonable amount of time, he will have to step aside from whatever ambitions he's pursued to support her in hers—even if he has yet to reach his destination.

This part is not easy.

Because there will always be something else that needs to be done, some other challenge that needs to be met, one more river that needs to be crossed before he feels like he's reached his goal. What he has to recognize, though, is that life just doesn't last forever, and that everyone has the right to live out their fantasies. What kind of man would he be if he hogged up all the prime time for himself and did nothing to help her get her chance to shine?

I say a loser.

I have a winner. Because after a year of watching Nick pursue his passion, I decided I wanted to pursue mine. In my dreams, I am Martha Stewart in blackface—an entertainer extraordinaire. I love to cook and I love to watch people enjoy my cooking. And now, I want to put writing aside, because while I enjoy doing it, it is not my passion. Entertaining is. And why shouldn't I get paid for doing what I love to do?

When I told Nick that I wanted to be a caterer, and save enough money to own my own bed and breakfast, he didn't balk. You know what my baby did? For my birthday, he bought me a food processor. Now, another woman might have been upset about getting a house gift on her birthday. I am an exception. Nick made my day with the Cuisinart—not only because he sliced my food preparation time into a fraction of what it used to be with my Ginsus, but because his gift choice let me know that he supported my dream to become a caterer and business owner. That, to me, was more special than any kitchen utensil anyone could ever give me, and that's saying a lot, because I love kitchen utensils.

It takes a sane, rational conversation and a well-thought-out plan to decide whose career takes priority—and compassion and understanding to know when it's time to step aside and let your partner pursue her goals. That means communication. And heart. And trust. And understanding. And most of all, lots of love to carry you over the humps.

Because there will be humps.

What would a woman have to do to get a man to accept that her career aspirations need to take top priority right now?

From a Brother

Frankly, it should be enough to tell him that she really needs to make a change to be happy. That would certainly be enough for me—as long as her request was within reason. When any of us find that one special thing that's going to do it for us, it's a travesty if another person's selfishness or self-centeredness prevents us from going for it.

The world is full of people who live their days on that human conveyor belt, like widgets at a factory. We wake up, go to work, find some way to make it through the day, come home, search desperately for a small bit of joy before we have to go back around the conveyor belt again. I've always gotten the impression that men are too busy making ends meet to worry about happiness. Or maybe it's because if we really were to sit down and think about the quality of our lives we might be too apt to flee the family and the job and the trap our lives have become. So we trudge along, forcefully steering our minds away from concepts like personal satisfaction. Movies like Brad Pitt's *Fight Club* and books like Susan Faludi's *Stiffed* have looked at the issue of male happiness—and received a considerable amount of flak for it. It's curious that though bookstores are filled with tomes on female happiness and Hollywood cranks out at least a few movies per month on women pursuing happiness, once there's an attempt to explore the male conception of contentment it's considered controversial and subversive.

As I write this I'm sitting here and listening to Curtis Mayfield's gloriously affecting and mournful CD *New World Order*, which he released a few years ago after he was left paralyzed by a freak accident during an electrical storm at an outdoor concert in Brooklyn. In order to record this majestic music, Curtis had to be suspended almost upside down to get enough volume on his singing voice. You listen to the result and you think about what he went through and you know what it means to find that thing that the Creator intended for you, the life's work that you would be compelled to continue even if you couldn't move. How many of us would ask to be wheeled into our offices or workplaces after getting paralyzed on the job and insist that we be allowed to continue working?

No, if my woman thinks she has found her passion, I am not going to do anything except get behind her and push as hard as I can. And then say a prayer for her fortune in finding it. I know there are people who say we weren't necessarily placed on Earth to be happy and that this obsession with personal happiness is a destructive American phenomenon of the late 20th century. They say the exorbitant divorce rate can be blamed on this obsession, as can our tendency toward grand, masturbatory acts of violence intended to exorcise those demons that make us sad when everybody says we aren't supposed to be. I'm sure there are many of us who interpret the quest for happiness to mean the hedonistic pursuit of gratification, the short-term high that is as permanent as a hit from a crack pipe. These people eventually discover their short-term gratification makes them feel worse when it's gone. But in the midst of our blooming divorce rates and frightening explosions of violence, this country is experiencing a level of prosperity unparalleled in the history of this planet. Maybe there's a connection between this prosperity and more Americans striving to spend their days doing the thing that will make them smile when they awake in the morning.

How many African Americans are in a position to pursue their life's passion? I would guess that there aren't many. Perhaps not coincidentally, we are not exactly full participants in the American prosperity. We scratch and scrimp, dragging ourselves to that damn job every morning with our blood pressure escalating at just the sight of the building. Many of us call it "the slave" and for good reason. It makes us feel trapped and unhappy and eventually it kills us. This is no way to live. This is no way to die. If our women or our men have an inkling of what it is that will lift their hearts and make them fulfill their full promise and glory, we have to have their backs. And who will be the ultimate beneficiary of the support that we give our mates? We will, of course. There's no denying the pleasure to be derived from living with someone who is satisfied with their existence, who is thankful to be in the place they are currently in. That person spreads their sunshine over their families and their loved ones like every minute of every day is noontime. And the entire family basks and flourishes in the power of those life-giving rays. We have no choice. We gotta have each other's back.

Infidelity: Should I Tell My Spouse?

From a Sistah

She thought she had done something.

My girlfriend was looking for a nanny to take care of her newborn once she broke down and went back to work. This is not an easy thing to do. You need someone you can trust with your child. Someone who will deal with her quirks, her crying, her messy, stankin', leaky diapers, her constant need to be held, her constant need to be entertained, her falling out when she can't, shouldn't, and won't get her way—her missing her mommy. Someone who knows that you will kill her with your bare hands if so much as a hair is mussed on your child's pretty little head.

This is a tall order—and it is not easily filled.

I told her that she needed to go down to her local church and find one of them old deaconess ladies with nothing but a closet full of big hats and a whole lot of time on her hands. That's the kind of woman who has plenty of experience with babies, a lifetime of old-time wisdom, and sense enough not to beat up on somebody's child.

Instead, girlfriend found a woman I'll call Juanita.

Juanita was a 25-year-old professional who was looking to work from home so that she could raise her own babies without the hassles of an office gig. To my girlfriend, Juanita was a sweet, mature mother who'd had obvious experience with children—both of whom girlfriend had met and found to be quite smart, polite, well-kept kids. "She's perfect," the chile squealed with delight. "I feel so much better now that I have someone I can trust to watch my baby."

It took me exactly five seconds to burst her bubble.

"Um, how old is she?"

"I think she's twenty-five," my girlfriend answered back, a question mark crossing her eyebrows. "Why?"

"Well, I'm not suggesting that something is going to happen, but are you sure you want a twenty-five-year-old single woman around your husband all day? I mean, shoot—that's just throwing a good man to the wolves."

Girlfriend was clearly puzzled. All she had been thinking about was her kid. But sure enough, we ran it past a male friend and he said I was right on point.

"She doesn't have to be cute," he said. "All she has to do is be there. Women are like cars to some guys; he might have a Benz sitting in the driveway, but every once in a while, he just may want to take the hooptie out of the garage and go for a ride to the corner store for a quick snack. No disrespect to the Benz."

Inherent in our male friend's response was that men are just going to cheat. Even a dumb, ugly gal can get your man to do it; all she has to do is provide the opportunity.

This, to me, is disturbing.

And disheartening.

Because I want to give men the benefit of the doubt—at least those I believe deserve it. And where I come from, there are a lot who do deserve it, my girlfriend's husband included. But I grew up with an older brother and his friends, and I watched them.

They'd be in solid relationships with beautiful women who deserved nothing but the best from their men—loved them, respected them, shoot, cooked for some of their sorry asses. And I know that these brothers loved them. But that didn't stop them from cheating on the women that they claimed to love.

And for the life of me, I can't understand how this can be. I mean, I feel like I've loved Nick for a lifetime, and I couldn't imagine life without him. The thought of losing him over some negro who could never, ever compare to him is just unfathomable. No man—not Maxwell, not Jesse L. Martin, not George Clooney, not even Brian McKnight—could change my mind on this, much less some hooptie I wouldn't be proud to take out of the garage and drive around the block a few times.

But, according to our friend, men are more than capable of such things, no matter how much in love they are—and the only chief concern they have with cheating is not getting caught, no matter how much they have to lose. Why is that?

If a man marries a woman and proclaims that he respects her and their relationship, why would he cheat?

From a Brother

Why do women cheat? Why does anybody cheat? Opportunity, curiosity, horniness, unhappiness, insecurity, jealousy—as you can see, the reasons are as plentiful as the number of synonyms in the thesaurus for the word bad.

First of all, whenever I see this question, it always seems to accept as a given that women don't cheat. But we all know that's not true. We all know women who sneak around on their men—in fact, many of the women reading this passage have done it. I've even been on the receiving end of the cheating woman, so I speak from experience. It may be true that men do it more often and more flamboyantly, but the finger can easily be pointed back at the females.

For men and women, we can boil it all down to a simple statement: People are immensely flattered by the amorous attention of the opposite sex. If you're around someone enough and you flirt with them enough, they will like being around you—assuming, of course, that you don't look like Quasimodo's lost brother (or sister). Certainly we can insert exceptions here—such as celebrities or people used to an inordinate amount of this flattering attention. But I'm talking about the average Joe or Josephine, who doesn't have their looks affirmed and celebrated on magazine covers and by throngs of screaming fans. The average Joe or Josephine can even be quite handsome or pretty. So handsome or pretty that you would expect them to get harassed every day just trying to walk down the street in peace. But even they will be entranced by the lavish praise and adoring attention of a co-worker or colleague who gets to do the flirtation thing on a frequent basis.

How Joe or Josephine responds to the flirting will vary, depending on a number of factors, but we can all be sure of this: Some of the Joes and Josephines will return the flirtations so zealously that they'll soon find themselves bouncing on some cheap mattress at a nearby motel, or on their knees in a supply closet. This will happen to many of these Joes and Josephines even if they go home to the world's most perfect mate and consider themselves madly in love.

For many of us, the lure of the flesh is so powerful that it can easily overwhelm some untested notion of fidelity that resides in our heads. It's like the picket fence that does a decent job keeping wayward leaves and trash from being blown into the front yard—then one day hurricane-force gales come along and toss the fence across the street. It takes serious and road-tested discipline to tame the monster that is the lure of the flesh. Not all of us have this kind of discipline. The ones that don't must pray that they aren't placed in situations where an attractive acquaintance decides to engage them in a prolonged dance of flirtation.

I suspect that one of the reasons more men are caught out there is because we are more likely to encounter single women who aren't shy about making themselves available to us and who don't seem to care that we're married or otherwise unavailable. These women come at us at the workplace, at the video store, at the gym, at the grocery store—hell, anywhere we might find ourselves without our mates. This is not intended as an indictment against all women because there are surely many of you who respect the ring on our fingers and don't try to lure us into anything we both know we shouldn't be doing. But for every four or five of these respectful women, there's the hootchie who just wants to have some fun and perhaps collect some trinkets in the process.

Perhaps if you traveled to some part of the planet where the single attractive men were much more plentiful than the single available women, you'd turn on the television set and see program after program of married men sitting around grousing about why their women insist on cheating. But here in our realm, a man is more likely to leave a married woman alone. That doesn't mean that if she's fairly attractive she won't have to fend off the usual lineup of men harassing her and calling out to her and all that nonsense. I'm talking about that sustained, slow-motion flirtation by a co-worker or a gym acquaintance whom she sees on a regular basis. Those acquaintances and co-workers are not likely to try to push the flirtation to the next level. Don't get me wrong—they will flirt. Everybody flirts. But they probably aren't flirting with a grand scheme already mapped out that ends with the woman at their apartment, bellowing at the moon while homeboy goes to work downtown.

I always thought it peculiar that companies like IBM and *The Washington Post* that implement anti-marriage policies actually think they are doing something to stop the distractions that sexual relationships can cause in the workplace. Haven't the human resources types responsible for these policies ever set foot on the floor of their workplaces to observe how much sexual tension and intrigue goes on in every square foot of the average company?

If companies really want to stop that kind of distraction, they should go out of their way to hire married couples. People would have to be crazy to cheat at the workplace right under their spouse's nose—which still doesn't mean it wouldn't happen.

If your inclination is to be suspicious of your husband's relationship with his pretty new secretary, your inclination probably isn't too far off base. But likewise for the fellas wondering why their wives are spending so much time working late on that big project with their handsome, rich boss.

What we're talking about here is cheating that leads to prolonged affairs, with torrid trysts in Holiday Inns all up and down I-95. But what about the one-night stand on the business trip, or the quickie in the coatroom at a cocktail party with someone we'll never see again?

If it was a little fling and it caused no harm, do you really want to know about it?

From a Sistah

Darling, there is no such thing as a little fling. Suggesting that a marriage would not be hurt by a man sleeping with a woman just a few times is no better than a woman saying she's only a little pregnant because she only slept with him once.

I can honestly say I'm disturbed by this question because it makes a "little fling" sound like the guy was walking down the street and some woman accidently tripped and fell on his dick. This, of course, is preposterous; if a man's penis finds its way into a vagina that does not belong to his wife, he is cheating.

Cheating can never be classified as a *little* sin. Adultery is adultery is adultery, no matter how you try to sugarcoat it. And in the mind of a woman—particularly this woman—a cheating mate is a clear sign of the worst kind of trouble in paradise.

Your keeping it to yourself will do nothing, in my book, but avoid the inevitable: the end of our relationship. See, if you found it necessary to stick your dick somewhere where it didn't belong, it's a sign that something is wrong with our relationship. Maybe I'm not sexy anymore. Maybe I'm a nag. Maybe you're tired of me. Maybe there's something wrong with you, and I've not minced my words in letting you know that I don't appreciate your crap. Whatever the reason, the fact still remains that all is *not* well in Denmark, and you are seeking something—whether it be peace of mind or simply pleasure—that you feel I can no longer provide.

Darling, there is no such thing as a little fling.

Because before you know it, that little fling is going to turn into a few more little flings. And then you're going to get sloppy. And then I'm going to find out, because, honey, we always find out. It's the perfume. The lipstick. The phone calls. The phone numbers. The time you spend away from home. The deafening silence between us. The kisses that have gone ungiven. The "I love you"s that have gone unsaid. The intimacy that has taken a backseat to something else—anything else—a baseball game, MTV, *Benson* reruns.

We will know. And if you survive the Bobbitting, you will certainly have to spend the rest of your life trying to prove to me that it will never happen again.

That's if I bother to stick around.

I wouldn't.

There are some women who would. But if they did stick around, you can, in the words of Don Cornelius, "bet your bottom dollar, baby" that she will never again trust you the way a husband should be trusted.

Because, darling, there is no such thing as a little fling.

In the back of her mind will remain the fact that, at some point in this relationship, you committed the ultimate marriage crime, and you will have to pay your debt to the wifey every day. You'll pay it when you walk in the door five minutes later than you should have. You'll pay it when you tell her you're going to play tennis with your boy, and you're gone for a few hours. You'll pay it when the boss sends you to another state on business. You'll pay it when you take her out to a restaurant and a beautiful woman looks at you, completely unaware that you are there with your wife. You will pay it every time the phone rings and there is a wrong number or a hang-up on the line.

Granted, it may just be a piece of ass for you.

But, darling, there is no such thing as a little fling.

Because the price is entirely too high. How much would it be worth to you? Are the kids worth it? Is the house worth it? Are the cars worth it? The money in our bank accounts? Me? Her?

It's certainly something to consider.

Because, darling? There is no such thing as a little fling.

We *will* find out.

Harm *will* be done.

You will not recover.

Would you want us to tell you if we cheated on you?

From a Brother

Where does this woman logic come from that says things like "that little fling is going to turn into a few more little flings"? When you enter womanhood do they give you a Bartlett's Book of Unproven Truisms *to repeat over and over in a jam because they sound like they might be true? I don't think there's any reason to believe that because a man has one encounter with infidelity it's suddenly going to become a lifelong habit. That's like saying if a man gets away with murder once, he's going to kill again (insert your own O.J. joke here). I just don't follow the logic. And for that reason, I'd have no reason to believe that my wife is going to cheat again because she did it once. Unless she's fallen in love with another man and is about to leave my ass, I say she should keep the story of her wandering poontang to herself. Let me remain blissfully ignorant.*

This is the kind of topic that gets weekly airings on the daytime television talk shows. Recently the crowd of women on *Oprah* all stood up and knowingly testified that you could tell when your spouse had cheated. "You just know," they said. "Or you know but aren't ready to admit it to yourself yet." I thought it all sounded like wishful-thinking bull. It sounded like the kind of stuff women say to each other when they want to infuse each other's souls with wonderful-sounding concepts like "empowerment." If you believe you can tell when your spouse cheats, then

188

when you go home and look into his blank face and see nothing but dopeyness—no signs flash across his forehead saying "Cheater!"; he wears no big scarlet *C* stitched into his oxford button-down shirt pocket—you think you're on top of this cheating thing because you see nothing. That theory sounds pretty lame to me. I saw a poll on America Online once that said nearly half of the more than 50,000 AOL subscribers who had taken the poll had cheated on their mates. With all this cheating going on, you'd think a lot more people would be getting busted if all we had to do was look our partner in the eye to make the discovery.

We know our women have a whole world of flirting and appreciative glances at cute guys and fantasies about the latest R&B star to flash across the screen. Not only would it be terribly unpleasant for us to be able to dive into this secret world, it would also be unwise. We should all be able to live the life of the mind out of the glare of watchful eyes—even if it's only one pair of eyes.

So, if I really love her and cherish our relationship and want her to be at my side forever, I most certainly don't want to know about her grabbing another dick on the side. That information would so permanently devastate me and haunt me that our relationship would have no chance of survival. The inside of our home would look like the aftermath of nuclear holocaust, with the survivors emerging from their hideouts and wandering around aimlessly in shocked disbelief at the extent of the carnage. No, I'd definitely need to escape this kind of emotional annihilation, even if it meant I'd never get to know about the smooth brother with the washboard abs who slid it to her from behind on that cruise when she was vacationing with her girls.

What I hear Denene saying is that a partner who has had sex with another person is necessarily making a statement about the quality of their marriage or relationship. I've heard that one before from women. It sounds to me like another quote from your *Bartlett's* book. Why does it have to follow that my lady is unhappy with me or with our sex life if she allows some casual flirting with another brother to escalate into her opening her legs in the heat of passion without thinking about the consequences? Like I said before, if she got enough flattering attention lavished on her by an acquaintance, she might be tempted to bite. She might not be disciplined enough to stop it before it went too far. She might be young or inexperienced with such talented or sexy suitors or just not mature enough to know what to do. I've seen it before. It's not as uncommon as the female gender would like to believe—or as your propaganda would suggest. She might want a little excitement outside the house; she might want to see what another man feels like. She might just be horny and the flirts came at precisely the right time. It happens. Just keep it to yourself.

16

Arguing: Does Someone Always Have to Win?

From a Sistah

L et me say this first: She does not like to argue.
Neither does he.

It gives her a headache. It works his nerves. It makes her angry. It works his nerves some more. Bigger headache. More nerves worked.

Still, sometimes it's simply a necessary evil—the end result of a serious discussion gone awry. One of them, usually her, will discover that there is a problem that needs talking about. They will each want the other to see—and agree with—their side. She, being the more talkative of the sexes, will want to examine all the reasons why there is a problem—a slow, laborious, energy-sapping process that no man's man likes. He will tell her she doesn't know what she's talking about, or, worse yet, try to simply solve the problem— end of discussion, with absolutely no input from her.

And before you know it, she's lost it. The reason? She has a need, driven by either her genes or a chemical reaction in her brain, to talk about it. She needs to dissect the action. She needs to know the motivation behind the action. She needs to know if the action ever happened before. She needs to know if the preexisting action had anything to do with the one currently being deliberated in today's sistah-girl court. She needs to know at least three solutions to said action. She needs to examine each of the solutions to determine which will best suit the situation. She needs to be cool with it. She needs to know he's cool with it.

None of this, of course, can happen without discussion. And sometimes, that discussion gets heated. And when it gets heated, it turns into a full-blown argument—the inevitable outcome of a sistah's quest to get to the bottom of thangs.

We think it is perfectly healthy.

You guys do not.

Which is why you all won't even discuss it.

Back to the headaches, the worked nerves, the anger.

I've never been very good at arguing. Get all tongue-tied and flustered and my mouth can never quite keep up with my brain, so the sane rational part of what I'm thinking usually doesn't get said—not in the heat of the moment, at least. What usually comes out is the hurtful things, the mean things, the hurled accusations meant to hurt my target. I usually don't like when my target gets hit, because inevitably, the target is someone I really care for. It's hard to reverse that hurt, hard to let go of the anger, hard to recoup. Lord knows that what makes words so incredibly powerful is that they can never be called back. Once they're in the air, they've invaded the space that we hold dear—the heart—and hurtful words, well, they do to hearts what a butcher does to a prime piece of meat.

So I would much rather not argue—will go out of my way to tiptoe around issues that just aren't worth the pain that they would cause if I did go there.

But some stuff just needs to get talked about, deciphered, decoded, and dissected—and damn if I'm not going to indulge myself. No, I do not get high from arguing. I'd much rather retire for the night with a smile on my face and my honey cuddled in my arms. Happy. But in a whole lot of cases, the arguments that I decide to have do solve a whole lot of problems; they've helped me get to the bottom of things, helped me to get my opinion heard, helped me to release my anger. This, coupled with the healing and some serious break-up-to-make-up action afterward, makes arguing worth the trouble every once in a while.

My relationship, see, is worth it.

All this is to say that I am like most women; we see arguing as a necessary evil in our quest to talk, and work things out.

Still, I can't count how many times a man has assumed and said aloud that we women argue—and will keep arguing—because we have a juvenile need to win. Win what, I have no clue, because at no time after any of my arguments have I received any prize. Just a cold shoulder until each of us got over whatever it was that we were arguing about.

I don't like cold food. I don't like bathing in cold water. I especially don't like cold shoulders.

Help us out:

Why do men always assume that a woman is arguing with them for the express purpose of winning?

From a Brother

There is no such thing as winning in these arguments—that's why we hate them so much. Never in the history of the human race has a man or a woman stopped cold in the middle of an argument and announced that their partner has won. We may think it, but we would never say it. After all, we can't have our loved one walking around thinking we can be dominated in an argument. That might make them too eager to do it again.

I had the misfortune in my formative dating years of going out with a philosophy major. In that relationship, our arguments would last forever, usually with me at least two or three steps behind as she quoted Nietzsche to prove one point, then Kierkegaard to buttress another. By the end, not only would I have failed to back up my position, but I would have no idea what she was talking about. Boy, that girl could argue. It's not surprising that she went on to become a successful attorney. What that experience taught me early and often was that it was folly to try to argue with women because we just weren't equipped with the tools for victory.

Furthermore, arguments seem to harden positions, not soften them. The heat of the moment pushes both sides even more deeply into their corners, where their intransigence will preclude any resolution to the disagreement. Usually things don't get solved until both parties have a chance to cool down and one side realizes that his or her position is flawed enough to hammer out a compromise—or plea bargain.

It should be noted that just because we ultimately decide to do what our woman wants doesn't mean that we agree with her. We may still believe in our position with just as much vehemence, but we know progress and peace will depend on somebody giving in to the other side. This requires a certain amount of inner strength and self-confidence. It is less important to us to be right than to allow the love and respect to flow through our relationship. We just go on ahead and buy the pink couch, or let her braid our son's hair, or let her go to the Maxwell concert without us so she can swoon and scream to her heart's content.

From my experience, it seems that men are better able to make these large, compromising gestures than are women. Our sense of self appears to be less connected to the outcome of the dispute (and maybe this statement will lead to a big, juicy argument—that I'll wind up losing). And this brings me to my most substantial point: What's the point of arguing when you're ultimately going to get your way anyway?

Women have too many weapons at their disposal for us to make much headway if we insist on winning. If we end the argument with some statement like "I'm not going to argue with you anymore. That's just the way it's goin' to be, dammit!" what have we really got ourselves into? We're probably going to be looking at days and nights of very little conversation, the chill reaching into every corner of the household; we're not going to have access to any poontang from now until perhaps the spring thaw loosens up her thighs a bit; we're going to find ourselves on line at KFC every other night for dinner, unless we have enough sense to grab some pots and pans and throw together some meals ourselves (we *should* have enough sense to do this, but that doesn't necessarily have any bearing on whether we do it or not); we'll realize how much cleaning our lady actually does around the house when we start finding things growing in the bathroom that we haven't seen since we prepared petri dishes in high school biology class.

No argument is worth the petri dish cultures.

We don't like to argue because someone's feelings always wind up getting hurt. Isn't that a good reason to avoid them?

From a Sistah

No—that's no reason at all to a sistah. She recognizes that someone's feelings are going to get stomped and that arguments are about as pretty as Whoopi in the morning. But she also recognizes that holding it in is so incredibly harmful that she actually risks hurting herself way more by not saying anything than she would had she simply gotten it all off her chest.

I once did a story about a wonderful book called *My First White Friend* by Patricia Raybon. What an awesome read it was—a memoir by an African-American columnist who grew up in a predominately white neighborhood in Colorado during segregation and experienced firsthand what it meant to be a dark-skinned black in America. She and her family and friends were hated by white folks—constant targets of hostility by ignorant people who just couldn't accept these African Americans as equals.

And while the author fought to retain her human dignity in a world that thought blacks were to be treated no better than a band of roaming stray dogs, she found herself constantly stressed, a condition that kept her medicine cabinet full. And no wonder; according to a 1996 study by the Duke University Medical Center and North Carolina Central University, racism significantly increased the risk of African Americans developing high blood pressure and heart disease. In the study, 30 healthy black women between ages 18 and 36 were asked to participate in two one-on-one debates with a white woman—one that was racial, another that was nonracial, but equally provocative. What researchers found was that their blood pressure and heart rates soared each time the white debater expressed racial opinions and the levels stayed high long after the debate stopped. They also found that the women had strong feelings of anger, resentment, cynicism, and anxiety—emotions that are associated with the dangerous stress hormones that can lead to life-threatening diseases like hypertension, asthma, and heart failure.

The researchers' conclusion: Racism can affect the physical and mental well-being of black folks, and the only way to stay healthy is to let go of the rage. It's exactly what Patricia Raybon did by her book's end, which helped her both overcome physical illnesses and get back on a healthy mental track.

All this is to say that just as Raybon and those black women in the study increased their chances for all kinds of jacked up diseases by harboring resentment and rage over racism, we too, I suppose, could do the same thing by harboring resentment and rage over our relationships with our mates. I know that there have been plenty of instances in which I've become upset over something that's gone wrong in my relationship, and the longer I've held in my feelings, the more enraged I've gotten.

We all know what happens when you hold back your feelings. Sooner or later, it's all going to pile up.

Really high.

And woe is the person who will be standing there when the dam breaks.

It's simply not healthy to avoid arguing to save someone's feelings, because ultimately, what you'll find is that no one really feels better—they're simply pushing the feelings down into this unsafe, dark, crowded space, where they will grow like weeds and fester like sores.

And then what?

I would argue that it's simply healthier for all involved just to talk about whatever it is that's on your mind. No, this is never, ever easy. Because at the end of the discussion, there's always the chance that someone is going to get pissed off at what is being said, or misunderstand it, or take it out of context. And the arguing will ensue.

The trick is to try to understand where your challenger is coming from—something that always helps in keeping a discussion from turning into a full-blown argument. And if this doesn't work—if you just can't avoid getting mad at what is being said—then it's important to learn how to let go.

Granted, we women have a serious problem doing this. But we can certainly try a little harder to understand that just because we're arguing doesn't mean I can't like you anymore—or love you less. It's just an argument. Tomorrow the sun will still shine, the bills will still need to be paid, and hopefully, my honey and I will still be together. But overcoming differences of opinion can't be something you *try* to do; you just have to *do it*.

Do men ever see a time when an argument is necessary?

From a Brother

You stay out all night and stroll back up in the house the next day with your makeup all messed up and your clothes askew? Uh, yeah, we will be arguing.

You complain to your mother about my failure to do enough housework to satisfy you? We will get our serious argue on.

You tell your girlfriend every little detail of our intimate moments together, knowing Wanda can't help but stick her fat ass all up in our business? Yes, we need to argue.

There are many occasions when an argument just can't be avoided, no matter how unpleasant they may be to us. In these instances, our anger will likely take over our better judgment and we wouldn't be able to stop ourselves from arguing even if we wanted to. You can be sure if you mess up you will be hearing about it.

I've always believed that how they respond to and recover from conflict is one of the most important issues couples face in establishing a relationship that has some staying power. Conflicts will come; somebody will mess up; we will make each other mad. What then? And after we fight, then what? Can we be strong enough to forgive, or do we hold the grudge like a notch on the belt—just waiting for the next screwup to feed on so that one day the grudge becomes so large and insurmountable that the relationship doesn't stand a chance?

Undoubtedly it is important to be able to vent our anger and frustration at each other. Black men suffer in even greater numbers from the various ailments you described before, often stemming from their having to deal with racism. Brothers should receive some type of medal when they get past age 60, in honor of their resiliency against the odds. Being able to vent to somebody will definitely help a brother get there. When one of my previous relationships started to go bad, a relationships counselor gave us a few exercises to work on that were intended to help the venting process and improve communication. We were urged to have venting sessions whenever the slightest thing bothered us. During the session, the offended party was to express their frustration or anger while the offender sat there without saying a word. When the offended party was finished, the offender had to repeat the reasons for the other's frustration, thus confirming that the other had been heard.

It sounded good on paper, but I soon discovered that I didn't want to do the venting sessions because they were just too damn stressful and painful. If my partner told me that she needed a session before the day was out, I'd be worthless the rest of that day. Forget about trying to get anything done at work—I'd become an ineffective bundle of nerves and anxiety. And even if I was the initiator of the session, I was still incredibly anxious about it. I suspect that my lady felt the same way because the frequency of the sessions quickly dwindled down to nothing. It wasn't that we didn't feel like investing the energy to save the relationship, we just wanted to avoid those damn sessions.

I think this is a microcosm of what men go through on a daily basis. The stress and strain of all that debate and argument is too much to take. We'd rather just let things slide and pray she doesn't do that again. Yeah, I know it's not the most effective strategy, but it's less stressful to us than the emotional roller coasters that come with argument and debate. We get enough stress from the rest of our lives. We want to avoid it at home at—nearly—all costs.

17

Dirty Laundry: How Much Do We Air to Friends and Family?

From a Sistah

She's our girl—so of course we're going to tell her stuff. She's the one, after all, who knows all our secrets, our inhibitions, our fears, our dreams and desires, our haunts. Girlfriend knows not only when we put that bone in the closet, but how big it was when we chucked it in there. And if she's really close to us, she probably helped us shove it in.

That, honey, doesn't change when we get a steady man. In fact, it only intensifies our relationship with her—mainly because she's probably the only objective ear we'll have if we're having man troubles and we need to get something off our chest.

Think about it: You all don't like talking to us about relationships. Treat it like the plague if we want to get into a conversation any deeper than, "Honey, what's for dinner?" Don't want to argue. Don't want to discuss it—in the light or the dark. Get bored with it.

And there's just some things I can't tell my mama and my daddy. I mean, the last thing I want them to think is that you're some trifling negro unworthy of their kid. So I'm not going to tell them you spent all our savings on a share in condos whose location, we recently found out, is actually Florida swampland. Or that you and I had a horrible fight last night and you went out drinking by yourself and came back into the house pissy drunk. Or that I think you might be cheating on me.

Because if I told my daddy these things, he would kill you with his bare hands.

And since I don't want you to die, I have to find someone else on whom I can unload my burdens. That would be my girlfriend.

She's the one who will not judge what we have to say. She's the one who will not get upset by what we have to say. She's the one who will agree with most everything we have to say. And when she doesn't agree, we will respect her opinion, because we know she's on our side and genuinely trying to help us understand and get over our problems. She will listen to us.

I treasure my intimate moments with my sister-in-law, Angelou, whom I consider to be my very best friend. We are both young and ambitious and intelligent and independent. We are both outspoken, but always careful not to hurt feelings or needlessly stir up ill will with our mates. We are both close to our parents, who are still married. We are both married to extremely handsome, intelligent, strong black men. And we both became mothers around the same time, to two of the most precious and loved children in God's creation.

You could say we have a lot to talk about.

And when we get together, we use each other to laugh and cry, and to complain about stuff that gets on our nerves but just isn't worth getting into with our men, and to figure out how to be better women.

There are, of course, some topics that are naturally off-limits. Like sex. And money to some extent. And sex. One could easily argue that these topics aren't discussed between Angelou and me because she is my husband's sister, and no sister wants details about her brother's sex life. I argue, however, that sex and money and a host of other topics just aren't anyone's business, much less Angelou's.

Regardless, I would think that my husband would appreciate this, seeing as Angelou is really releasing him, at times, from needless arguments and countless confrontations.

This, however, always seems to get lost on men, who assume that we're telling our girls all the juicy details of our relationships. I will make one concession: Some of us ladies do not know what is appropriate banter for the girls, as opposed to what's not.

If you could draw the line for us, where does sharing our problems with our loved ones end and airing inappropriate dirty laundry begin?

From a Brother

As I see it, there are two issues here: substance and tone. Not only does it matter what you say, it's also important how you say it. The Academy Award–winning dramatic performances have got to go— you know, when you call up your girl and say, all loud and offended, "Girl, you wouldn't believe what this negro did last night!" So even if you proceed to tell her we got into bed with unclipped toenails and one of them left a little scratch on your leg at some action-packed point in the night—of course, you wouldn't tell your girl about that now, would you?—she will pick up your clues and decide that we are the most disgusting creature she's ever had the misfortune of meeting. That's about tone.

As for substance: Sex problems are off-limits. You ladies *do* know that, right? You simply are not to talk about any difficulties we are having in the bedroom with anybody else, particularly if you want to assign the blame to us. You should not be giving any of your friends enough information to sketch a mental picture of anything we do in the privacy of our bedroom. Period. There are very few exceptions here. We know you ladies blatantly violate this one on a regular basis, but that doesn't make it right.

For instance, there's a couple who live not far away from us in New York City. From all indications, they are a fairly nice couple, except they have a problem. The wife is no longer interested in sex. From what I've heard, part of the problem is that the hubby ain't got no skills. (They have two children, so he must have been allowed to enter the precious portal on at least two occasions.) His cluelessness has drained all interest from the wife, who is quite pretty and sexy in her own right. So far I'm sure this story doesn't sound outrageous or atypical, but there's one thing you should know: I've never met this couple. How do I know about their problems? Because the wife has a big mouth! She's been yapping to so many people about their bedroom problems that the information has somehow made its way through the gossip grapevine to me, a complete stranger. Now, how jacked up is that? If I ever have a chance to meet this couple, what am I supposed to think as I shake the hubby's hand? Will it even be possible for me to have any respect for this fellow, for our relationship to start out without my preconceived notions clouding everything up? Probably not.

This is man's greatest fear—that there is information about his sexual proclivities and performance problems floating out there in the ether, accessible to strangers and, perhaps even worse, close friends. Because I can say from experience that it's real hard to take a man seriously when we know he "can't work the middle," in the words of Puff Daddy. He becomes a laughingstock to us, a joke. We may two-facedly smile up in his mug, but as soon as he's out of earshot the snickering begins. It may sound awful or mean, but it's true.

There's also another danger here—when women give information like this to other men, they sometimes use it to get to the good stuff themselves. I know because I've done it before. In my younger days when I was working at a newspaper in Dallas, I worked out at a health club where the front desk was run by a lovely young lady with whom I began to develop a casual friendship. When I was done working out, we played the little flirting game, all in innocent fun. She wasn't the brightest porch light on the block but she was friendly—and sexy as hell. Soon she started sharing intimacies with me that got my ears all big. She started telling me how her husband just couldn't satisfy her in bed, that he was mean to her and she just didn't know what to do about her marriage. I would shake my head in sorrow and tell her it was a shame that someone so young and pretty was not having a satisfying sex life. She would agree that it was indeed a tragedy. Then one day I had to add another line, an experiment to see how she'd react.

"If I was married to you, I'd have you baying at the moon," I said, all cocky and obvious. I wasn't really expecting this woman to cheat on her husband—but that's exactly what happened. By the following month, homegirl had become a regular visitor to my apartment, where she was able to confirm that her husband didn't know what he was doing. I don't know if their marriage survived— we drifted apart after about two or three months—but she certainly didn't help matters by sharing their private problems with me. And I certainly didn't help matters by responding the way I did—although in retrospect she might have been playing me all along. It wasn't my finest hour, but I use it to illustrate my point: Sex talk is off-limits.

Unless we haven't eaten for a week and we're starting to look longingly at that can of cat food, money problems are off-limits, too. We don't need the whole world pitying us for the sorry state of our finances. And we don't need any handouts either, unless we ask for them. Nothing worse than walking around with everybody thinking you're a broke-ass good-for-nuthin' negro.

You might object to my use of the expression "the whole world" above, but it wasn't an empty phrase. If you tell your girls about our problems, there's a high probability that a large percentage of our world will know about it by lunchtime. Sure, you might begin the confession with one of these: "You can't tell anybody . . . "; "Promise you'll keep it a secret . . . "; "If I tell you, you absolutely *can't* tell anybody else . . ." Of course she nods her head or whispers into the phone that your secret is safe with her. You can practically hear the slobber dripping from her lips as she's greedily preparing to receive the juicy morsel. Keep your secret? Shoot, you'd have a better chance of getting Janet Jackson to sing at your wedding. At the risk of boring the populace by reintroducing the whole Clinton-Lewinsky debacle, I have always wondered whether homegirl actually thought she could tell two dozen of her closest friends and not have the whole world—and this time I mean it literally—find out about it.

Our delicate medical problems are off-limits, too. If we're buying Depends because of our recent bouts with incontinence, do we really need your family and friends staring at our ass everytime we get up from the couch?

There are a few exceptions to this privacy rule. If you are talking to your girls to get advice or counseling for your own problems, then go right ahead and yammer away. We all know your girl Lisa is a freak mama extraordinaire, so I got no beef with you calling her up to get some lessons to improve your various techniques. If we've been plagued by your sudden frigidity, a long discussion with your friend Sharon might be just the elixir we need to get you, uh, moving again.

Why do ladies run to their friends at the first sign of trouble anyway? Can't you handle your problems yourself without calling a national sistah-girl conference?

From a Sistah

Mental release. Strategy. And so that we won't stab you in your sleep.

It's really quite that simple.

I don't know about other women, but I do sometimes have a problem talking to my husband about things that I know are going to bring discord to our household. Ironic, huh, particularly since we write relationship books and seem, by all accounts, to be able to talk to each other about anything.

Well, let me be the first to hip you to some life game: It doesn't matter how open your relationship, how comfortable you are with your mate, there are going to be times when you just won't want to get some mess started. You will avoid the confrontation like the plague—sleep on it, dance around it, bury it beneath some other mess that is less painful. But you will never quite get to the part that is bothering you the most, because you know it's going to stir up some stinky, nasty, sticky shit.

Needless stinky, nasty, sticky shit.

Like the time I'd held in for way too long the fact that I thought Nick didn't really spend enough time with our daughter. I mean, I'd be in her room with her from sunup until way past sundown, nursing her, singing to her, reading to her, dancing with her, playing with her, napping with her, and hours would go by before he would even stick his head in the door to see if we were dead or alive. And when he did check on us, he never once offered to take her off my hands for a little while, to give me a much-needed Mommy break.

Now, don't misunderstand me, here; I absolutely adore spending time with my child. But being a mother is way more than a full-time job. Shoot, at least in a full-time job, you get a half-hour lunch break and extra dough for overtime—so long as your union dues is paid up.

But in my house, this just isn't the case. I can't count how many times I just haven't had time to pee, much less grab a bite to eat, because I was simply too busy with the baby to take even two minutes of time for myself. Which wouldn't be so bad if I didn't have to walk into the dining room and see my husband leisurely reading the *Times* while he eats lunch, or walking on the treadmill while he watches BET or playing Madden 2000 on the computer when I thought he was in the room working hard on his book projects.

How liberating, I'd say to myself, to know that you can do what you want to do whenever you want to do it with no worries about diapers and fussiness and continuous entertainment all day every day. Then I'd just get pissed.

But Lord, the day I said something about it, we ceased all communication for about a week. Because he thought that he was pulling his baby load. And I didn't. And we just couldn't agree. Not even to disagree. And I simply couldn't get him to see my side of it.

We eventually got over our funk, but I'd still get burned up when I'd see him bent over a plate of food while I was trying to get the kid to sleep. Still, I didn't want to invite another argument—another seven days of silence. So I'd quietly stew until I could get a free phone minute to talk to my girlfriends. And, as usual, they all understood exactly what I was talking about because they, too, had gone through the same exact child-rearing thing with their mates.

My release? I got to get off my chest exactly what I needed to get off it, without getting into a big blowup with Nick over it. Clearly, there was no winning this disagreement with him, and I thought it was more important to avoid the confrontation because it didn't really fill my need to have someone—anyone—to understand that I just didn't like his way of doing things.

It was with great relief that I came to understand that I was not alone in my frustration—that Nick was no special breed of man. Each of my mommy girlfriends had similar experiences, and each of them had gotten into arguments with their mates about it. Nick and I are normal, after all.

The strategy came in their helping me to understand how to handle the situation: Either get used to it, or give her to her daddy and leave the vicinity so that he'd put in his time, my girls told me. "Don't bother arguing with him, because you're not going to win this one," my girlfriend Cathy advised. "But if it gets really frustrating, you should try talking to him calmly about it," my girlfriend Carrie reassured me. "Girl, one of these days, she'll take two-hour naps and you'll get to do what you want to do," Angelou told me. "Hang in there."

It was helpful, sound advice—advice that kept me from grabbing up the Ginsu and cutting my husband. This, darling, you should appreciate. The girls saved you. You should be thanking them, rather than getting upset because I talk to them about you. Ha.

Do you guys ever talk about your problems to your guy friends?

From a Brother

If we're lucky enough to have a friend with whom we go way back, yeah, we're going to discuss some of our problems with him. But there is an obvious line that we do not cross, even with our boy. We'll talk about money problems we're having and medical problems we're having, but we won't talk much about sexual problems. Besides, even if we did tell our boy every little detail, there's one key difference here: We can keep a secret.

After all, that's what this comes down to—you tell things to people whom you can trust. At least that's what we do. I can't speak for you ladies. If y'all had to judge your true friends by the ones who you were sure could keep your secrets, y'all would be some lonely, friendless ladies. At least that's the way it appears from the male perspective.

Our boys can be extremely helpful to us—particularly since we're usually so reluctant to reveal any personal matters to the outside world. When I was going through the ache of a divorce, it was my friend Shawn Dove—who had recently gone through the same thing himself—who talked me through much of the pain. It was crucial to my sanity to have someone around who not only understood the difficulty of divorce but who knew me so well. And when we both met new women who proved to be joyful salves for our damaged souls, we were both able to truly enjoy each other's good fortune because we had been there for the lowest times. I know it's not every man who has a friend that valuable. Unfortunately, we place so many barriers between ourselves and other males that we have a hard time reaching out to another man when we are in need. It's part of our screwed-up notion of manhood, a useful, working definition for which many black men are still waiting.

I think men spend their lives in need of meaningful connections with other men, but we really don't know how to establish the strong, intimate bonds that will help to sustain us. We set everything up between men as competition and rivalry, not helpfulness and understanding. But those of us who have close male friends know how much strength we get from them.

Look at Vernon Jordan and President Clinton. They go back for decades and it's clear that their bond couldn't be tighter. When Monica Lewinsky told her best friends—all 89 of them—about her dalliances with the world's most powerful man, it wound up igniting a scandal and provided the special prosecutor with lists of people he could call as witnesses who had heard firsthand from Monica. On the other hand, the prosecutor got squat from Bill's best buddy. You know Vernon was intimately familiar with every tiny piece of dirt that Bill has created over the years—and you just know there were plenty—but ol' boy will never give it up. Bill knows he will never give it up, which is why he can continue to rely on Vernon as his best friend. They have each other's trust.

Everybody felt contempt for Ralph Abernathy for dropping the dime on Martin Luther King's sexual indiscretions just to sell some books a few years back, but at least old Abernathy waited three decades after the stuff went down to open that curtain. He probably could have sold a lot more books if he had done it 20 years ago, but he waited until the stories were so old that he had to blow dust off them before he cracked them open.

However, even with our best friends there's no need to give details of our sex life with our love partners. When talk rolls even close to that topic, we will offer up vague details—enough for the brother to get the point without needing to draw a mental image. In the movie *The Best Man* by Malcolm D. Lee, that was the one subject that almost tore apart the rock-solid friendship of Morris Chestnut and Taye Diggs—whether Diggs had been with Chestnut's wife-to-be. Even our boys know that they have to stay away from that subject if the friendship is going to survive. I bet there's very little Vernon Jordan could tell you about Hillary Clinton's bedroom proclivities. He might know every facial tic Monica makes when she's on her knees performing a service, but I would guess he has about as much information on Hillary in bed as the rest of us.

18

Who You Calling a Bitch?: Does It Matter How We Talk To Each Other?

From a Sistah

So, tell me, are they giving men How to Be a Complete Idiot to Women 101 classes somewhere, or is it just something in the Y chromosome? Because for the life of us, we women don't get why guys continue to think that talking to our boobs and shouting obscenities at us when we don't respond and calling us bitch and treating us like we're video hos is a turn-on.

Yeah, yeah, yeah—talk that stuff while you're walking with "well, if you would act nicer, maybe brothers wouldn't have to call you out your name."

Uh-huh.

She could be the mother of your child.

And a Sunday School teacher.

With a disposition as sweet as Aunt Jemima and her syrup.

And the personality of Mother Teresa.

And guys would still find it necessary to call us anything but a child of God.

And let her decide not to respond to his behind, or open her mouth to let him know she doesn't appreciate being disrespected. Then she will have clearly invited the really special words—*bitch* and *ho* and *chickenhead* and *pigeon*—words that assure her that this guy certainly deserves her attention. Down at the police station.

Let me hip you all to something: Calling her something other than her name at the top of your lungs is not a woman's idea of a smooth way to keep her around—make her feel special.

Ignorance of the aforementioned will simply make her blood curdle. Hello? You're her man. And you just said something really rude and inappropriate to her—something even a dog doesn't deserve.

If you're calling her this, chances are that you might not have a problem taking this a step further, like raising your hand and striking a blow each time you call her rude and vile names.

So excuse the hell out of her if she ignores you—or runs like hell.

This rationale, though, is not readily accepted by men. In fact, when I wrote a column on the same subject for the *Daily News* a few years back, my words invited a host of vile letters from people who dared to call themselves men, each of them riding me for taking offense at the names and comments I've received on the street and, in some cases, in my very own home from men who clearly didn't deserve my time or attention. One went so far as to tell me that I'd probably hand over my digits to the guy with the foul mouth if he had on a nice suit, because that's just how superficial we women are.

I thought this was extremely unfair, and you know I let him know this, too—in a five-page letter I'd directed to his attention.

Still, it amazed me that men just don't get it: The quickest way to get yourself dismissed is to call a woman other than her name. So answer me this: Why do men think it's okay to call a woman everything but her name—whether he's trying to get her attention on the street or plain mad at her?

Does anybody ever teach men how they're supposed to talk to women?

From a Brother

Unfortunately, this is one of the things we learn by example. That is a notion that should scare us all, especially considering what young men see these days.

I was lucky: I had my father as a model for my behavior in this regard. I could watch the way he talked to my mother, how gentle and peaceful and considerate he has always been around her. He was the best role model I could ever have in this area. Even when they argued, he'd never really raise his voice and he certainly wouldn't say anything that was rude or disrespectful. I assume he didn't do any of these things when us kids weren't around because, if he did, I think the attitude—if not the nasty words—would carry over to the arguments they did have in front of me and my two sisters.

It's a good thing I had my dad because what I saw around me growing up was mostly hostility and insults between the sexes, whether it was family and friends or the images that marched across my TV screen. The family that lived next door to us included three girls and three boys, all close enough to my age and the ages of my two sisters that we became as tight as can be. The things I saw go on in their house between the mother and father used to scare me half to death. Their father was a mean, angry, brooding man who became even angrier at the world after he had been drinking. He was a star athlete in high school and things had been downhill from there. He was filled up with hostility that came flying out of him at just the slightest provocation. Apparently, his wife provoked him a lot. To me she appeared to be one of the sweetest, kindest women I'd ever been around. This woman always had a smile at the ready and she seemed to carry around none of the anger you'd expect from an abused woman. The only time I'd see her raise her voice was when her husband was beating on her face. And I saw him beating her on quite a few occasions. I can't even imagine the level of cravenness that would move a man to beat up his wife in front of not only his kids, but his kids' friends. Here I am up in their house with my G.I. Joe collection trying to get my play on, and the crown prince of Hades would stagger in and proceed to drag us all on a dark journey through hell. He'd scream and curse at his wife for the smallest, dumbest things and then start swinging. I had never seen grown folks fight except for the boxing matches on TV so I was horrified and fascinated at the same time. She'd be crying, the kids would be crying, stuff would be falling onto the floor. I'd be hiding behind the couch along with the other kids. So much for the so-called superiority of two-parent households. A few years later, the middle son—the one with whom I was the closest—committed suicide. Thanks, Dad.

How about those black TV relationships? What were the most popular black shows during my formative years? *The Jeffersons*, *Sanford and Son*, *Good Times*, and a few others. Think about the way that Fred Sanford talked to the women in his life. And wasn't it nice the way George and Weezy Jefferson got along, the kind and loving manner in which they addressed each other? Yeah, right. George Jefferson was about as loving as his former neighbor, Archie Bunker—how about Archie for a model of how to talk to your lady? In other words, television wasn't exactly full of positive images in this regard.

There's so much natural contempt between boys and girls as we're growing up that we both have to achieve a major mental about-face to treat each other kindly and talk to each other with respect as adults. It's not easy; most of us need help, guidance. It always made me squirm when I would hear guys around me refer to females in disparaging terms like "bitches" or "hos," but it wasn't until I reached adulthood that I would dare utter a scolding word to the brothers. Most teenagers don't have that kind of self-confidence; I surely didn't. What I would do instead was find a reason to excuse myself and proceed to avoid those guys if possible. I just didn't get it—it was almost as if they hated the very same creatures that they spent practically every waking hour scheming to spend time with. I went away to college assuming that the harsh disparagements of females would stop because it was the domain of low-class ghetto negroes. For the most part I was right—I ran into very few brothers at Yale who would work their mouths to call women "bitches." But every once in a while I'd stumble across a few brothers using the same terms I thought I had left back in Jersey City. It happened so seldom that it was shocking, but it happened enough to tell me that you could take the brother out of the ghetto, but you couldn't always take the ghetto out of the brother.

In her infinite wisdom, my mother always used to tell me that it was the common courtesies that made us civilized, and nowhere were those common courtesies more necessary than at home with your family. She would say this after I snatched something away from one of my sisters without saying "please" or "thank you." Her words stayed with me, though, as they usually do. When I got into relationships of my own, I'd be offended if my partner forgot these common courtesies when we were together. I was surprised by how often it happened, too—I'd find myself with women who seemed to take for granted the little things I did for them. If I went into the kitchen and brought them back a glass of water, I'd expect a "thank you." Not much to ask, right? It shows me that you appreciate the effort. If I make you dinner, I expect you to be as grateful as I am when you make dinner for me. Every time I do you that favor and I don't get a "thank you" in response, you know what happens? It makes me less excited about doing it the next time. It makes me feel underappreciated, like you think it's my job to serve you. Of course, it's incumbent upon me to show you the same courtesy when you do something for me. It has to go both ways, otherwise the neglected partner may start thinking he or she should go elsewhere to find a little more appreciation.

I've heard it said that common sense isn't common—well, the same can be said about common courtesies. Even when we have disagreements, that's no reason for politeness and respect to fly out the window. That's when it's even more important for us to be polite to each other. It's sometimes hard to abide by that when the anger has reached the boiling point, but it's when we let go and allow the tongue to start flapping that all kind of unpleasantries come pouring out that we can't take back. Martin Lawrence did a hilarious stand-up routine about how black women quickly throw the harshest, nastiest insults they can find at their men during arguments because they know the man isn't (hopefully) going to take a swing at them. Many brothers won't even respond in kind with the name-calling because they've been taught better than that—

after all, our mothers might find out. But sometimes we might slip up and let one of those bad words come sliding out if we get really pushed. We wince right as we hear it falling from our lips because we know the world will come tumbling down on our heads like an imploding building once the word is out there.

How come you can call me names, but when I call you one, it's a sign of the coming apocalypse?

From a Sistah

Because words are the only weapon we women have to wield against men who really deserve an ass whippin' that we're not strong enough to give, whereas when a big, burly man starts hurling insults at us ladies, it can easily be taken as a serious sign of aggression—the kind of aggression that could lead to bodily harm.

Oh, your words will make us want to draw blood from you—just like Queen Latifah did in her song, *U.N.I.T.Y.,* in which she kindly tells a guy not to disrespect her with that "Yo, baby" lest he get punched "dead in his eye." Lucky for you guys, though, the woman you called a "bitch" because she rolled her eyes at your air kisses isn't Queen Latifah. No, the one you just disrespected will simply ignore you because she knows—and you know, too—that she doesn't have the power to say anything back. Face it: What woman wants to tell a big, burly six-foot-two guy he has no right to comment on the shape of her butt, the bounce of her breasts, the length of her skirt, the tightness of her top, her dislike for hurtful words and foul names? Some might dare to tell him off, but most will simply ease their way past him and pray to God he doesn't keep pushing the issue—because a little woman is no match for an insult-spewing guy who could easily flick her like a flea.

I think this is why guys spew lewd comments at women as they make their way down the street or when they get upset at their women in the household. They know they can. The travesty is that these guys are the same fools who are surprised when women don't immediately fall to their knees, thank the Lord for sending such a fine gentleman their way, and excitedly hand over their phone numbers or stick around when the fight is over.

At worst, you could be an ax murderer—at best, a woman-beater ready to physically abuse his prey. So we are especially cautious of the man—if you want to call him that—who would not only raise his voice toward a woman, but call her a vicious, hate-filled name. Instinctively, we'll duck to avoid the expected blows.

But our name-calling? You can pretty much expect that that's all you're going to get from us. Most of us—save, like, the prison-bound chick named Bertha and all those she-women who take home the trophies in those greasy weight-lifting contests—don't have the muscles or brute to go toe-to-toe with a man. So we'll do what we can to get as close to his nerve as possible, without having to go to hand-to-hand combat: We'll curse him out like he stole from our mama and smacked our child.

And it feels good, too. You ever see those stories about "yell therapy," in which people are encouraged to just howl like a banshee? You see these fools standing in the middle of empty rooms, just screaming at the top of their lungs? There's something to be said for it. I mean, it's a serious release—to be able to say just what you want to say as loud as you want to say it to the person who has worked your nerves the worst.

Unfortunately, this could be you. I'm not strong enough to beat you down, but damn if I can't curse you out. You know how they say a dog's bark is worse than its bite? Well damn if that bark doesn't make you think twice about stepping to the owner.

Whether it's on the street, in private with your boys, or in our homes, why do black men seem to have such hostility for black women?

From a Brother

I question why we both have so much hostility for each other. I certainly can feel the male hostility for the females, but I also feel quite a bit of it the other way, too. This is like the unanswerable conundrum—which came first, the chicken or the egg? At this point it doesn't even matter which came first. The real question is, can the mutual hostility be lowered—and how?

I must admit that I don't have much hope when I turn on the radio and the television. The song lyrics have become increasingly confrontational, more mocking and disparaging of the opposite sex than ever before. I laugh and shake my head—then I remember that this stuff is being sucked up by our children, who are taking it all in like sponges. What are they to think of it all, having little to give them any perspective? It's one thing to hear *Bitches Ain't Shit But Hos and Tricks* and dismiss it as cartoonish nonsense—though I'm sure there were plenty out there who sadly took Dr. Dre's words to heart—but another to hear Destiny's Child instruct women on how they are supposed to view relationships by talking about a man paying their bills. That is much harder to dismiss because it's a philosophy so many women take to heart—apparently including my wife, who does enjoy quoting her Destiny's Child lyrics and was overjoyed to get their CD in the mail. What's the message that we have to fight against wherever we turn? Men are banks and women are hookers. Not very uplifting stuff, is it?

It's become almost clichéd in our community to complain about the explicit and damaging content of hip hop music and videos. We keep complaining and it seems only to get worse. If anybody's listening, they only take the complaints as cues to make the stuff even harsher the next time—after all, controversy sells. Nothing better to sell a record than to make it piss off some grown folks, right?

But then I spend time around actual teenagers and I'm a lot more hopeful. For the past five years I've been teaching a writing class on Saturdays in a Harlem-based program called Legal Outreach. The program tries to use the law as a motivational tool to push kids to college and beyond, with the goals of big dollars and the societal acceptance that a law career can bring. James O'Neal, a dear friend and the program's executive director, has the highest expectations imaginable for these kids, no matter what neighborhoods they come from or what their family situations look like. O'Neal doesn't suffer fools or excuses gladly. Many of the students go to classes all summer and every other Saturday during the school year. I'm around more kids at *Harlem Overheard*, a youth newspaper for which Denene and I have served as editorial directors for the past three years. Created and run by dear friend Shawn Dove, another taskmaster, these teenagers spend many of their weekends toiling away in the newsroom on news stories, editorials, profiles, and columns about young people and the Harlem community. In both programs these teens are typical New York City high school students—they like their hip hop, they complain about getting too much work, they sometimes forget to study, they can't stop thinking and talking about the opposite sex. And they are as respectful and protective of each other as you'd ever pray high school kids could be. The boys usually show courtesy when they speak to the girls; the girls aren't hostile or dismissive when they speak to the boys. Watching them interact with one another gives me hope that the dangerous and destructive messages they hear in the music and see on their television screens aren't getting through—or if they are, they aren't being interpreted as rules to live by. Their music isn't rendering them unfit for successful, respectful relationships later on down the line. It's not making them play so many games with their expectations of each other that they really don't know how they should expect to be treated by the opposite sex. These kids and their interactions remind me of the ways my friends interacted 20 years ago, of the ways teenagers have treated each other for generations.

I wonder if things will change for these teens by the time they reach adulthood and start seriously dating. Will they become jaded and pessimistic like so many in our community, made bitter by experience so that all hope and expectation is beaten out of them? Or will their optimism and good cheer stay with them? How do we mold more kind and courteous kids like them? Are they a pre-selected group of more responsible, intelligent kids because they choose to be involved in academic and intellectual pursuits on Saturdays and summers when they could be doing a million other things? Are they that different from their peers?

Kids imitate what they see. If they see adults treating each other with respect, they will do the same. If they see fighting and hostility, that becomes their model. If they spend time around other kids who know what it means to be courteous and kind, that's what they will become. Instinctively we all know this stuff—though many of us don't put it into action when we have an opportunity to model behavior for young people. We get much more carried away with our own bitterness, like the single mother who just can't seem to stop herself from calling the kids' father a "stupid asshole" every other day in the presence of the kids. We selfishly settle into our own pain, like the teacher who counsels the young girls under her wing to stay away from boys as long as possible because they will only cause heartache and suffering—just as they did the teacher.

For so many of us who once may have been those bright-eyed teenagers, the challenge remains to keep the cheer into adulthood, after we have endured a string of ugliness and negativity with the opposite sex. Everyone has had negative experiences with the opposite sex. No one has a patent on heartache and suffering. It just goes with the territory—part of growing older and wiser. Just as we've all met members of our own sex who have made our lives a little more depressing and nastier by their existence, there's nothing to stop those same miserable souls from bringing their brand of misery to members of the opposite sex, making it that much harder for the next positive brother or sistah who comes along just looking for a smile and a kind word. I know that I won't attract the kind of people I like to be around if all I show to the world is gloom and doom. So I tell myself to smile as much as possible. Give people a little bit of warmth. It doesn't cost me anything. Because after a while, turned down too many times into a nasty frown, my mouth will forget how to do anything else.